SURVIVING A CYBERATTACK

SURVIVING A CYBERATTACK

*Securing Social Media
and Protecting Your Home Network*

Todd G. Shipley
Art Bowker

MERCURY LEARNING AND INFORMATION
Boston, Massachusetts

Publisher: David Pallai
MERCURY LEARNING AND INFORMATION
121 High Street, 3rd Floor
Boston, MA 02110
info@merclearning.com
www.merclearning.com
800-232-0223

T. Shipley and A. Bowker. *Surviving a Cyberattack: Securing Social Media and Protecting Your
Home Network*
ISBN: 978-1-50152-312-0

The publisher recognizes and respects all marks used by companies, manufacturers, and developers
as a means to distinguish their products. All brand names and product names mentioned in this book
are trademarks or service marks of their respective companies. Any omission or misuse (of any kind)
of service marks or trademarks, etc. is not an attempt to infringe on the property of others.

Library of Congress Control Number: 2024943515

242526321   This book is printed on acid-free paper in the United States of America.

Our titles are available for adoption, license, or bulk purchase by institutions, corporations, etc.
For additional information, please contact the Customer Service Dept. at 800-232-0223(toll free).

All of our titles are available in digital format at academiccourseware.com and other digital vendors.
The sole obligation of MERCURY LEARNING AND INFORMATION to the purchaser is to replace
the files, based on defective materials or faulty workmanship, but not based on the operation or
functionality of the product.

To all those tirelessly battling the darkness that preys on the vulnerable through fraud and abuse—this book is for you, in recognition of your courage and commitment to justice. Educating others about fraud has been a lifelong endeavor.

CONTENTS

PREFACE

The authors, with a combined investigative experience of over 50 years, aimed to create an easy-to-understand guide for the general public to prevent and survive cybercrime. This book, consisting of ten chapters, is the result of their efforts. Both authors have successfully trained law enforcement in cybercrime techniques, even those with minimal computer skills. The book is written in a way that anyone with basic computer skills can understand, while also providing helpful information for advanced practitioners. Readers will benefit from the included checklists for applying the book's steps and principles. The chapters are written to be stand-alone references for the reader, and it is not necessary to read the book all at once, cover to cover.

Chapter 1: Cybersurvival Versus Safety

Explains that cybercrime is a fact in today's world and is the first step to understanding how to begin to protect oneself when using the technology around them. It discusses the crimes committed through technology and the places criminals target victims.

Chapter 2: Digital (Cyber) Security Basics.

Introduces readers to the risks of connecting to the Internet, especially with the rise of Internet of Things (IoT) devices. It offers practical advice on ranking and mitigating those risks, emphasizing the importance of a properly configured router. The chapter includes checklists for router setup and tracking the devices connected to your network.

Chapter 3: Safely Going Online

Explores the various hazards users face when accessing the Internet and provides actionable steps to minimize those threats. It covers the essentials of secure browsing, managing cookies, using antivirus and antispyware software, and securing connections with VPNs and Wi-Fi. It also clarifies the important distinction between privacy and security.

Chapter 4: Securing Social Media

Covers the risks posed by social media platforms and provides strategies for protecting personal data online. From creating and maintaining secure passwords to adopting strong security habits, this chapter equips readers with the tools needed to navigate social media safely.

Chapter 5: Protecting Children

Focuses on the specific vulnerabilities children face in the digital landscape. It offers guidelines for approving devices and managing the associated cyber risks to ensure young users remain safe.

Chapter 6: Protecting Adult Family Members

Examines the unique challenges of caring for vulnerable adults who may not be equipped to handle online threats. It provides strategies for protecting them from cybercrime and outlines steps to address social media after a loved one passes.

Chapter 7: Surviving in the Online Marketplace

Highlights the risks of online shopping and trading. Offering tips on how to identify threats and protect yourself while navigating the digital marketplace in the modern age.

Chapter 8: Protecting a Small Home Business

Provides critical advice for small home businesses (SHBs). Covers a wide range of topics including protection from scams, data security, social media management, and employee computer monitoring, helping SHB owners secure their digital assets.

Chapter 9: Surviving a Digital (Cyber) Attack

Prepares readers to respond to a cyberattack by revisiting key prevention strategies from earlier chapters and offering additional guidance on how to survive and recover from an attack.

Chapter 10: Future Trends

Discusses emerging trends in digital security and offers insights into what the future may hold for both individuals and businesses as they continue to face new and evolving cyber threats.

T. Shipley
A. Bowker
July 2024

ACKNOWLEDGMENTS

I would like to thank my entire family, my wife and daughter, and especially my parents who could have benefited from it.

Along the way, I have been influenced by many who have dedicated their lives to fighting fraud.

James "Jimmy" Deal, a friend and fellow fraud fighter was always there and was always encouraging me to stay in the fight

Todd G. Shipley

I would like to thank my children, Stephanie and Mark, and my grandchildren, Scarlett, Raylan, Vivian, Margaret, Owen, Felicity, and Abigail— may this book contribute to creating a safer online world for you and future generations.

Art Bowker

To ensure this book would be a valuable resource to the public we solicited input on draft chapters from parents or individuals who had professional experiences dealing with certain populations, such as vulnerable adults or cybercrime victims. We are thankful to the following individuals' comments and suggestions for improving our book: Maryum Ali, Tim Barry, Stephanie Burlison, Bonnie Burthker, Jeff Coyle, Julie Delaney, Anitra Merrett, Danielle Mahoney, Jack Riffle, Michael Sullivan, Rich Threadgill, Rachel Yokely, "Big Ashes," John Cryer, CFE, and Erin West, Esq.

CHAPTER 1

CYBERSURVIVAL VERSUS SAFETY

IN THIS CHAPTER

Understanding that cybercrime is a fact in today's world is the first step to understanding the need to protect oneself and family. This chapter provides up-to-date numbers and historical data on major cybercrime events and provides an overview of the cyber-risks we all face.

Modern humans are a connected species. The Internet has made this possible, providing communication and information access few could have envisioned when it went commercial in the late 1980s. Unfortunately, our information highway also connects the world's criminally inclined to countless unsuspecting and unprepared victims. Cybercrime impacts us all, and the odds are pretty good that individuals, including children, will face cybercrime attempts/acts multiple times throughout their lives. (Figure 1.1)

Many cybercrime studies are anti-malware vendor-supported and focus on the dangers of an unsecured personal computer, mobile phone, or device, which those vendors hope will translate into product sales. These are serious concerns, and one is foolish not to protect their devices. Nevertheless, it is naïve for people to believe that simple antivirus and antispyware software and firewalls will protect them from all the cyberdangers present in the twenty-first century. These basic measures are just the starting point of digital age survival.

Significant data breaches over the last ten years, such as those experienced by Target (2013), Sony (2014), Anthem (2015), OPM (2015), Equifax (2017), Microsoft (2020), and Facebook (2021), were not attacks on individual users but on companies entrusted with users' data. Once the attackers gained information, they either used it themselves for malicious purposes or sold it to others, who used it to victimize individual users via identity theft or other financial crimes.

It would be nice to think that all individuals must do is avoid shopping, working, or getting services from companies that think cybersecurity is a low priority. How does one determine that before they are victimized, and their data is stolen? People could all start shopping at a store like *Hee Haw*'s Gordie's General Store, which had no computer or Internet vulnerability, but that is not today's reality. Additionally, with

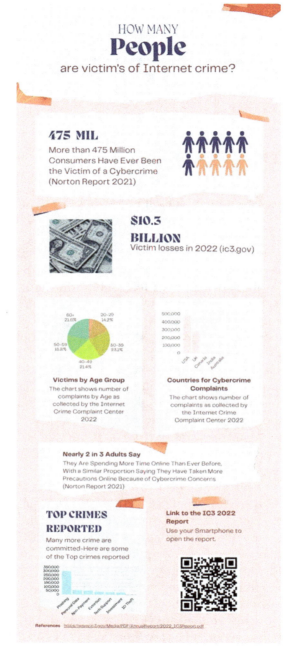

FIGURE 1.1 Number of victims of Internet crimes [FBI, 2024].

some organizations, there is no choice. People must deal with them. Of course, the organizations we are referencing are government agencies that have not established an impregnable cyberfortress. In 2014, the State Department, the White House, the National Oceanic and Atmospheric Administration, and the United States Postal Service joined the long list of hacked government entities. These pale in comparison to the 2015 breach of the Office of Personnel Management (OPM). This significant breach included the background information on government employees who applied for security clearances. Like so many others, both volume authors received OPM letters identifying them as data theft victims.

The information in this book is advising you how to avoid victimization, not just from the authors' perspective as law enforcement investigators, but from their own experience as victims.

Users expose ourselves even when they don't deal with an organization for services. Countless individuals have established social networking profiles, frequently without considering the security or privacy settings. They share information with others, believing those they communicate with are who they purport to be. People erroneously convince themselves that what they post will not be shared with someone they don't approve. People often erroneously trust their relatives, friends, and associates not to forward their information to others or they believe that their security/privacy settings are locked down. With all these misconceptions, people also believe that social media sites have security that prevents them from being victimized. Unfortunately, the wealth of information these sites contain makes them a tempting target for those criminals looking for information that can be converted into something of value, such as access to someone's bank account. Social media companies are not immune to cyberattacks. In 2013, hackers stole two million passwords from social networking sites, such as Facebook, Twitter, and LinkedIn, and email providers Google and Yahoo. Being the CEO of the largest social media company does not make one immune from being attacked for poor password usage. Facebook founder Mark Zuckerberg had his Twitter and Pinterest accounts taken over due to his reuse of passwords that the hackers found in a dump of stolen passwords from business social media giant LinkedIn in 2012.

Attacks are also literally coming from every direction and device. Thousands of unsecured webcams in the United States and Western Europe provide footage for a Web site based somewhere in the Russian Federation. An extreme privacy invasion, these unsecured webcams can also be used to determine the best time to commit a robbery or burglary. Webcams are not the only vulnerability. One security expert correctly observed that our coffee pots, televisions, stoves, and refrigerators are enabled on the Internet, and their security protocols are not always adequate. How does one avoid an Internet risk that is increasingly being built into common household devices? Recent reports have noted certain modern vehicles have been hacked and the discovered vulnerabilities allowed actors to control car functions, such as starting and stopping.

In the early days of computing, Gene Spafford director of the Computer Operations, Audit, and Security Technology (COAST) Project at Purdue University opined, "The only truly secure system is one that is powered off, cast in a block of concrete and sealed in a lead-lined room with armed guards - and even then I have my doubts." Spafford [1989] Today, we live in a society where everyone must be concerned about not just their own computer or system but everyone's. The reality is the world is such that no matter how safe one makes their computer and their personal practices, someone else may drop the ball and expose them to cyberharm. If it is not a company, an agency, or a "friend" on social media, it is a coffee pot or refrigerator leaking information to the world.

To make matters worse, cybervictimization is not just limited to having personal identifiers and credit/finances stolen or privacy invaded. There are other, more sinister harms awaiting the cyberpublic. Sexual exploitation of children has long plagued the Internet. Child molesters regularly visit teen chatrooms looking for victims. Bullying and stalking are increasingly occurring online, with 10% to 40% of youth experiencing cyberbullying. Sextortion, a form of blackmail where the criminal uses sexual explicit images of the victim to gain financial reward or worse, has resulted in not only financial loss but numerous suicides. Some murderers, and more specifically, serial killers are using the Internet to hunt victims.

Cybercriminals often use social engineering techniques to convince victims to part with their finances. The Internet Crimes Complaint Center (IC3) reported the losses reported due to investment scams in 2023 became the most of any cybercrime tracked by them. According to IC3 investment fraud losses rose from $3.31 billion in 2022 to $4.57 billion in 2023, a 38% increase. As reflected in Figure 1.2 investment fraud victims were often over the age of forty. Figure 1.3 shows that all reported IC3 crime losses significantly impacted the older population. The cyberthreat clearly does not diminish as people get older [FBI, 2024].

Safety or protection implies one is free from danger or harm. We can minimize and maybe avoid it, but the access made available by the Internet is not free from danger or harm. The term cybersurvival is much better. It recognizes that there is danger or harm but has a connotation that goes beyond safety or protection to overcoming those attacks.

The goal in writing this book is not to make users "unplug" and refrain from using the Internet. Being an ostrich in a digital world is no way to live. The authors will draw on their collective cyberlaw enforcement experience to not only maximize readers' ability to avoid being a victim but also to prepare readers in the event they

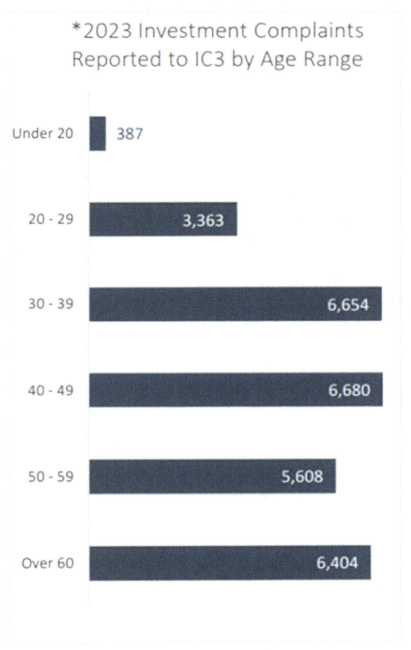

FIGURE 1.2 IC3 investment complaints by age range.

2023 - COMPLAINANTS BY AGE GROUP [13]

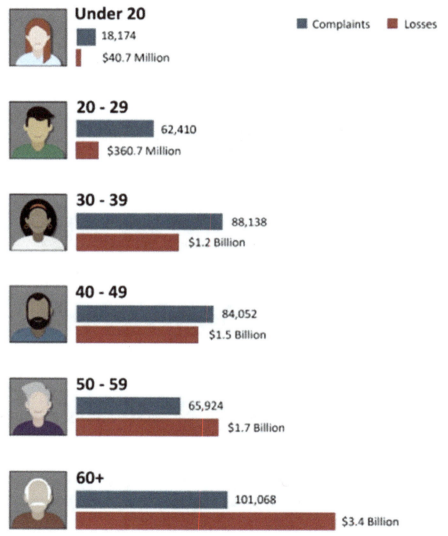

FIGURE 1.3 All IC3 complaints by age group.

become a cybervictim. The goal is to enable readers to survive in a world where cybercrime events are becoming an everyday occurrence. The authors will provide information on how to strengthen cyberdefenses and recognize and avoid cyber risks. They devote specific chapters to protecting children, vulnerable adults, and small businesses. They also provide readers with information on how to be safe in the online marketplace. They will educate readers on minimizing the harm if they become a cybervictim. Finally, the authors will educate readers on how to properly document and report a cyberattack to law enforcement to maximize the potential for the perpetrator to be apprehended and prosecuted, hopefully making everyone safer in today's digital world.

The authors will accomplish these goals by simplifying concepts and not inundating readers with technical jargon. When they do use technical information, it is explained. The authors have collectively educated and trained law enforcement on these concepts for years, and they know how to explain things to individuals who do not possess a degree in computer science or security. For those with a computer science or technical background who happen to pick up this book, the authors hope it is a valuable resource for explaining things to loved ones who are less technically advanced.

CONCLUSION

Understanding that cybercrime is a fact in today's world is the first step to understanding how to begin to protect oneself when using the technology around them. This chapter discussed the crimes committed through technology and the places criminals target victims. The next chapter will begin the journey of understanding how to protect oneself and the technology used at home and in the small-business environment.

REFERENCES

Federal Bureau of Investigation (2024). Internet Crime Complaint Center. "2023 Internet Crime Report," April 21, 2024. *https://www.ic3.gov/Media/PDF/AnnualReport/2023_IC3Report.pdf*

Gene Spafford (1989) "Quotable Spaf" *https://spaf.cerias.purdue.edu/quotes.html#:~:text=The%20original%20quote%20is%3A%20The,'Reilly%2C%201997%2C%20S.*

CHAPTER 2

DIGITAL (CYBER) SECURITY BASICS

IN THIS CHAPTER

This chapter discusses the risks of connecting to the Internet and provides suggestions for ranking those risks particularly as they relate to Internet of Things (IoT) devices. The key to mitigating those risks, the use of a properly configured router, is also covered. Additionally, included are checklists for router configuration and documenting the devices that connect to the Internet.

CONNECTING TO THE INTERNET

Ease of use is how devices are valued. Users expect things to be simple to operate and want them to work the first time without much tinkering. Computer advances have historically strived toward simplicity. An example is the graphical user interface (GUI) that allows users to operate a computer without typing commands. Plug and play also allows a new device to start working immediately when connected to a computer. Simplicity is built into today's technology. Simplicity comes with a hidden cost, namely security.

Today, Internet access requires two things: a device (laptop, desktop, tablet, cell phone, etc.) and an Internet service provider(s) (ISP). It is simple. Internet access in this manner is like freeway driving with no brakes and no seat belt. This chapter will discuss how devices connect to the Internet, the associated risks, and how to prioritize security.

EARLY COMPUTER CONNECTIVITY

Initially, computers and all their associated devices were connected via cables or lines. These devices included mice, keyboards, printers, scanners, and, once upon a time, a modem. The modem was connected to the Internet via a phone line, and in turn was connected to the computer via another cable. If the home user didn't have a modem, their computer couldn't connect to the Internet.

In the business setting, things were a bit more complex. Computers often connected to other computers, some of which were called routers, and acted as communication traffic cops. The more tech-savvy home user had a router, particularly if they had more than one computer in their home network. Routers will be discussed in more detail later, but their functionality allows several computers to "share" another device, such as a printer or modem. Early Internet connections, even in the business and home network setting, required a modem to connect to the Internet.

In the late 1990s, modem functions moved from an external device to an internal computer component. Users plugged their phone line directly into a "port" on a computer to have Internet access. ISPs began expanding the types of service offered beyond "dial-up," such as digital subscription lines (DSL) and cable. These additional service types did not require an outside modem but merely plugged into a computer via a "converter" and then into a computer port. Those remaining dial-up ISPs were accessed by the telephone line plugging directly into a computer port. External devices, such as printers, scanners, and routers, still required cables connected directly to a computer in order to function.

In the early 2000s, wireless arrived on the scene (Figure 2.1). No longer did a computer have a wire connecting it directly to a device, such as a printer. Computers could connect to a modem via radio waves or a Wi-Fi router. A wireless router is still connected to the user's Internet connection via dial-up, DSL, or cable ISP via a line. Even that was to change. Starting with cell phones, computers could go online via a wireless ISP. Wires became a thing of the past.

FIGURE 2.1 Wireless access.

During the transition to wireless connections, the ISPs came up with a device that combined modem functions with that of a router. This combination modem router allowed numerous computers in the home to connect to the Internet through one connection. This provided the home user with immediate access to the Internet from any device they allowed to communicate to their combination modem/router. These new devices were built to facilitate worry-free connecting for the typical home user, however, built-in security measures were lax. Additionally, the home user has limited access to modify the device's settings to enhance security. Some devices have the access code fixed to the device's bottom. Any visitor to the home, such as a repair person, babysitter, and so on, needs only to turn over the device and take a picture of it, and they have the access code required to get on the wireless network. Additionally, ISP providers don't always keep up with security updates and patches on these devices, making them vulnerable to hackers. Just such a vulnerability was discovered in AT&T's DirecTV Linksys wireless video bridge [Whittaker 2017]. Home security of these devices continues to be an issue. (See Figure 2.2.)

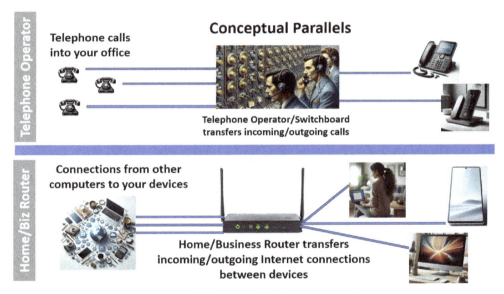

FIGURE 2.2 Conceptualizing how routers work.

THE ROUTER IS THE GUARDIAN

As previously discussed, routers are like communication traffic cops due to their ability to share network resources (communications) with other devices. They do much more than that. They provide an additional layer of defense between your computer(s) and hackers.

For a device to connect to the Internet, it needs a unique Internet protocol (IP) address, which an ISP supplies. That IP address is provided to other computers during activities such as sending emails, browsing, and so on. If one does not use a router, that IP address becomes a direct connection for an attacker. In a real sense, it is like providing an unpublished telephone number to someone so they can harass the person on the other end at will.

Routers are the first line of defense. An attacker must bypass the router before they can even start attacking a computer(s). Routers use the same IP address provided by the ISP to connect to the Internet. It "filters" communications to computer devices under its protection by providing local IP addresses, which are not visible to the Internet. Communication comes into the router, which decides which device should receive it, and then forwards it based on the local IP address it assigned. A properly configured router does not broadcast these local IP addresses or how many devices it serves.

Compare it to an old-time switchboard operator at a hotel. Incoming callers are never told who is staying in which room. The "call" goes to the router (switchboard operator), who then forwards it to its intended recipient (room) based upon rules for such communication; for instance, no calls forwarded after 9:00 p.m. If the communication is deemed a threat or not allowed, the router does not forward it to the device.

Routers frequently have firewalls that restrict incoming as well as outgoing communication. Others have firewalls that control communication between devices on the network. In this way, a compromised device, such as a printer, could not be used to gain control of another device, such as a computer.

Routers can also provide parental controls or restrictions for certain devices. These controls can include the inability to access the Internet during certain times or prohibitions against specific Web sites or Web pages with text that violates certain standards (explicit language or too much profanity).

Some routers support virtual private networks (VPN), which allow users to connect to specific networks remotely, such as a home user connecting remotely to their business network. Routers also monitor network usage and can send email or text alerts when something starts to go look suspicious. In this way, your router becomes an early warning system for trouble.

THE FIRST LINE OF DEFENSE

What type of router should one buy, and how much should they spend? Choosing the right router can be a challenge because one wants the best product for a reasonable price. The issue is that technology changes so quickly that it's hard to recommend a make or model without the advice being almost immediately stale. There are some specific things the Wi-Fi router should do to protect your home network.

Commonly, a major concern is with the range at which one can connect to the Wi-Fi router (e.g., does it cover the whole house?) and the speed at which one can get data when connecting. From a security standpoint, these are the last things one should be concerned with regarding our router. Most new routers are plug-and-play. The user must log in to the Web-style interface and go through a wizard to set it up. A software wizard or setup is a user interface that guides the user through a series of steps to configure a program. It simplifies complex or unfamiliar tasks by breaking them into smaller, manageable parts and is usually quick. Let's take a look at the things you should look for when buying a Wi-Fi router for home use.

1. *Standards, standards, standards:* Don't get confused by the long list of standards such as 802.11g, 802.11n, or 802.11ac. They are written technical standards of a router's capabilities. 802.11 is the official standard name, and the trailing letters are the revisions. The newest standard available is preferred for the average home user. Don't buy old technology, as the newer standard will be superseded soon enough. Users should not risk their network by buying something old. They should purchase the most current version. Users can ask the sales clerk at a technology store or search Google for "current 802.11 standard."

2. *Multiple band routers:* When looking at routers, users will find most modern routers broadcast on multiple bandwidths. Typically, the 2.4GHz and 5GHz bands make it convenient to surf one band and stream video on another.

3. *To MIMO or not to MIMO:* Multiuser or MIMO is a technology that allows many devices to get a high-bandwidth Wi-Fi signal simultaneously. It distributes the data more efficiently over multiple connections, giving users faster Wi-Fi speeds.

4. *Security:* Wi-Fi networks are popular but can be insecure. Users must secure their home network to prevent hackers within range from eavesdropping. To do this, one must consider what security means in the Wi-Fi context. There is a list of mind-numbing acronyms about security features. They are listed as follows starting with the most secure and ending with the least secure:
   a. WPA3
   b. WPA2 + AES
   c. WPA + AES
   d. WPA + TKIP/AES
   e. WPA + TKIP
   f. WEP
   g. Open Network (no security at all)

Remember that the network will only be as secure as the least safe device connecting to the network. That means phones, tablets, computers, or other devices connecting to the Wi-Fi all need the same level of security to make the network secure. The highest current security is WPA3. *Wi-Fi protected access* means the second implementation of the WPA protocol. Select the highest level of protection available for every device added to a home network. As of 2018 devices must also support the WPA protocol. The letters such as +AES after the protocol are the level of encryption used with the protocol.

WPA3 Personal is the newest, most secure protocol currently available. It will work with devices that support Wi-Fi 6 (802.11ax). Older devices might work with the newer protocol. The older security level WPA2 might be acceptable, although not ideal. Sometimes only one protocol is available and that is one that must be used. Look into purchasing a newer router with the latest protocols. Refrain from relying on the oldest standard, wired equivalent privacy (WEP). The oldest standard is easily broken with free downloadable tools making them inherently unsafe to use. In Table 2.1 we have some basic recommendations for the suggested Wi-Fi protocol to use for personal or home use.

TABLE 2.1 WIFI Suggested Protocol Use

Protocol	Recommend?
WEP-Wired Equivalent Privacy	No
WPA-WIFI Protected Access	No
WPA2- WIFI Protected Access 2	Only if newest standard of WPA3 is not available
WPA3- WIFI Protected Access 3	Yes

5. *Logging:* This feature is essential as it lets one know if someone is targeting the network. In worst-case scenarios, logging can provide important information about the *timing* and nature of a security breach.

6. *Other features of interest:* These can be nothing more than fluff, but they can be helpful in the right circumstances. A USB port on the router can add things like backup space for devices. These same features also present a potential security liability. (As an example, if the system is compromised, it's possible the data in the backed-up files might be, as well.)

7. *Cost:* Ultimately, the cost will be the primary driver in the purchase. After deciding on a budget, users should choose a router that fits their needs, as the most expensive ones may not always be the best option. The right Wi-Fi router should have essential features that will protect a home network. Cheaper, subpar routers can be dangerous and expose the network.

Now that readers have a better understanding of what they should look for when selecting a Wi-Fi router, the next step is buying one. There are many different options, going to a local big box store and talking with a knowledgeable salesclerk can be valuable. Searching on the Internet for reviews of devices is also an option. The final purchase decision is a personal one based on one's understanding of the product.

Provider Modems with Wifi

Service providers sometimes offer the option to have Wi-Fi enabled as a service provided by their equipment. This sounds good, but the issue is a matter of control. Users may not have control or access to the security functions within this device. The best approach is to have the service provider turn the Wi-Fi function off and add the preferred WiFi router and control after they service the device. Table 2.2 provides the home user with a basic checklist to guide a home user when setting up a Small Office and Home Office (SOHO) router in their home. This is a guide and some of the various steps will be dependent on the make and manufacturer of the router being installed. Use this a guide to set up your SOHO router.

TABLE 2.2 Router Setup Checklist

	Task	Completed
	Required Items: A) wireless router with power cord B) two **Ethernet** cables C) computer or laptop	
1	*Plug in the router and turn on the router.*	
	Connect the Internet modem to the router. Plug the Ethernet cable into the router Ethernet port named "WAN" or "uplink" or "Internet."	
2	*Turn the modem off* and turn it back on (This is to ensure the router is recognized).	
3	*Connect a computer to the router.* Plug an Ethernet cable into the computer's network connection and the other end into an open port on the router.	
4	*Open the router's administration tool.* Open a Web browser on the computer connected to the router. Check the bottom of the router or installation manual for the IP address. Often, the default address is http://192.168.1.1 or http://192.168.0.1.	
5	*Log in to the router.* Enter the default username and password (Provided in the router's documentation).	
	Make the following suggested changes to your router. The location within the routers will vary. These changes will help to secure your router from misuse by others.	
A	*Change default administrator passwords (and usernames).* This is of utmost importance. Changing the admin username and password prevents users from accessing the router and making changes.	

	Task	Completed
B	*Turn on encryption.* If this function is available, consider using it to further harden access by users (but understand its function and how and where the keys are stored before implementing).	
C	*Change the wireless network name;* this is often called the SSID. Don't use the default name. Make it unique so that it is easy to remember. This is the WiFi name one's computer sees and connects to.	
D	*Enable media access control (MAC) address filtering—or access control.* You can use this function to control the devices with access to the router. A MAC address is a physical address associated with the computer's network card or other device. Do a Google search to find steps to obtaining the devices' Mac address. Using this allows only those MAC addresses the user enters to utilize the router. (Most modern routers will provide a list of the devices and their MAC addresses to allow on the network.)	
E	*Assign static IP addresses to devices.* This is another security feature that prevents unknown devices from entering and using the router. With this function, one can assign an internal IP address to each device they allow.	
F	*Disable SSID broadcast* after the password is changed and the WiFi connection for the router is named. A important security feature is to turn its broadcast off. If it's not broadcasting, no one knows it's there. Only the user knows the name and password, so only they can access the router's WiFi.	
G	*Turn off Ping return.* Most routers have a function to respond to requests called a Ping that identifies if they are online. Turning off this function hides the router from certain Internet threats that are using the function to identify targets for attack.	
H	*Enable a firewall on router (if installed).* Some modern routers have additional features, such as a firewall whose function is to add security to prevent access to a network, therefore it's important to them.	
I	*Turn on the Internal security logging.* Logging of security events on a router, in most cases, is turned off by default. Turn this function on to record and make any security event or unauthorized access to devices available for later review.	

NOTE *The information contained in this table is a general guide, and the steps will vary depending on the router's make and model. Always review the manufacturer's installation guidelines for details.*

Once these steps have been completed, verify the computer can connect to the router and the Internet.

INTERNET OF THINGS (IOT)

The Internet of Things (IoT) is a term adopted to denote all devices that connect with the Internet with unique identifiers. It covers not only computers but any device that can communicate via the Internet. The list is constantly growing and can include medical devices, industrial, construction, or farming equipment, household appliances and environmental controls. Why is this a risk? First, these devices typically have either no security or very lax security features. Second, these devices are becoming more and more a part of life. For the general public they can include anything from a home thermostat to a child's talking doll, or a pacemaker. The vendors who sold these devices may not have disclosed their security risks. Hackers have used seemingly worthless IoT devices to breach high-value targets. In 2018, a group of hackers used a fish-tank thermostat in a casino to steal a high-roller database. Any IoT devices can pose a possible security risk. Becoming aware of the risks is the first step to becoming more secure and being able to take action.

HOW DOES ONE SPOT THE CYBER RISKS?

Identifying cyber risks can sometimes be an overwhelming task. In today's world, any device connected to the Internet at any time can potentially be compromised and personal information can be exposed. Many of us remember being cautioned about our world's potential dangers as children. The admonishment, "Don't talk to strangers," is one of the more common warnings we heard as children. It was an attempt to help us be safe in an unpredictable world and avoid the issues of people unknown to us. We taught our children the concept of "stranger danger" and don't take candy from strangers.

Few could have predicted the digital dangers awaiting us, particularly as they did not exist when Baby Boomers were growing up. Early Generation X, citizens born between 1965 and 1980, were either young adults, teenagers, or preteens before the Internet truly took off with the 1990s public arrival of the World Wide Web. Few of their parents or teachers had any idea how to use a computer, let alone be prepared for the developing digital dangers.

The Millennials (born between 1981 and 1996) faced a similar problem as few of their parents had acquainted themselves with even the basics of digital safety. In short, we have a society where brick-and-mortar threats, such as stranger danger, were drilled into us, but the digital hazards of modern society are only now starting to be stressed. Another problem is that digital hazards seem to be constantly changing or evolving. It seems that with each new technological innovation, some criminal adapts it for a nefarious purpose.

What Is Our IoT Risk

For clarification this section will look at this from a risk potential versus actual harm. The worst-case scenario is that all IoT devices are capable of being hacked and taken over. If a hacker can take over the device, what can they accomplish with that control? Can they expose personal information or threaten children's security?

Risk might be viewed on a continuum, with each device having all the risks associated with devices attached to it. Consider it as a potential risk as a device used to launch an attack against another device and possibly control that device. Does the device itself have the built-in hardware to accomplish some objective, that is, spying or controlling some function at the location (temperature, locks, air, and lighting)? Can the hacker's control cause the device to set an electrical fire or some other damage? Table 2.3 is a list of the Four Levels of IoT Risk the a person may find with the IoT devices in their home. You can use this to understand the possible risk you have in your home.

TABLE 2.3 Four Levels of IoT Risks

Risk Level	Description of IoT Risk
Low risk	This level encompasses IoT devices that do not handle sensitive or personal data, and their failure or misuse does not pose a significant threat to individuals or organizations. Examples of these devices include smart home appliances, fitness trackers, and environmental sensors.
Moderate risk	Devices in this level may pose a moderate risk to individuals and organizations. These devices may collect personal information, such as health data or financial information, but have limited access to sensitive data. A breach of these devices could result in the exposure of personal information or disruption of services.
High risk	IoT devices at this level have the potential to cause significant harm or disruption if compromised. They may have access to critical infrastructure or sensitive data, and a breach could have severe consequences. Examples of high-risk IoT devices include medical devices, industrial control systems, and smart cars.
Critical risk	Devices in this level pose the highest risk to individuals and organizations. They have access to highly sensitive data and are integral to the functioning of critical infrastructure, such as power grids, transportation systems, or water supply systems. A breach of these devices could have catastrophic consequences, including widespread disruption of services and potential loss of life.

NOTE *Be aware even an IoT device that can't get access to sensitive data can still be used to provide information about user habits. For instance, a low-risk device such as smart home appliances or fitness trackers could, if compromised, let hackers know when one is regularly home or where they might be at a given time.*

Checking Devices for Home Security Risks

Users should have a general understanding of what devices they have at this point, and they may be apprehensive about the insecurity of their home technology. It's helpful to break the items into separate functions, note their particular use, and map out one's home network. Use Table 2.4 to start mapping the technology in your house.

1. Determine what devices allow access to the Internet in the house. These will generally be routers provided by one's service provider or ones the user has added to the home network (see the section on protecting routers).

TABLE 2.4 Digital Risk Checklist

	Your Digital Risk Checklist	Answer Questions here	
1	How do you access the Internet from home?	For example, this could be wireless or an Ethernet connection.	
	Who is the Internet service provider?	E.g., This could be the cable provider.	
2	How many routers are in the house serving up WiFi connections?	Each one can be a weak point or possible access to the network.	
3	List below all of the technology in the house that has access to the Internet or connects to another device.	E.g., computers, cellphones, your car, cameras, baby monitors, appliances, etc.	
	A List of My Technology	Serial Number/Markings	Connection Type
A	E.g., Mom's cell phone		☐ Wi-Fi ☐ Bluetooth ☐ Wired Ethernet
B	E.g., Dad's computer		☐ Wi-Fi ☐ Bluetooth ☐ Wired Ethernet
C			☐ Wi-Fi ☐ Bluetooth ☐ Wired Ethernet
D			☐ Wi-Fi ☐ Bluetooth ☐ Wired Ethernet
E			☐ Wi-Fi ☐ Bluetooth ☐ Wired Ethernet
F			☐ Wi-Fi ☐ Bluetooth ☐ Wired Ethernet
G			☐ Wi-Fi ☐ Bluetooth ☐ Wired Ethernet
H			☐ Wi-Fi ☐ Bluetooth ☐ Wired Ethernet
I			☐ Wi-Fi ☐ Bluetooth ☐ Wired Ethernet
J			☐ Wi-Fi ☐ Bluetooth ☐ Wired Ethernet
K			☐ Wi-Fi ☐ Bluetooth ☐ Wired Ethernet

2. Look at the devices that attach to this router wirelessly or by Ethernet cable. Ethernet cables are inherently more secure connections because they are direct connections through the cable. Wi-Fi is less secure because it uses radio waves that can be intercepted. Our section on protecting one's router discusses features to mitigate this insecurity.

3. Most IoT devices will connect to the Internet through one's WiFi connection on their router.

    a. Each device comes with instructions about how to connect it.

    b. Identify the login procedures for each device.

    c. Login into the devices one at a time and identify the security function available for that device.

    d. The most often overlooked security for IoT devices is changing the admin names and passwords; change these immediately.

    e. Consider using the MAC filtering function in the router and assigning internal IP addresses to the IoT devices.

Table 2.4 should include all family members household's devices, including cell phones, iPads or tablets, computers, and home routers. There are other things to consider. For example, what about one's car? Does it connect wirelessly to their smartphone? Refrigerators, nanny cams, security cameras, GPS devices, home thermostats, or any other electronic devices that connect wirelessly to a home network can pose security risks. Record the make and model, serial number, and any identifying marks of such items (this could help the police if the items are stolen and also for insurance purposes).

Once one has an inventory of these things, they can better determine the risk of potential unauthorized access to their homes. If some devices are mobile, new risks will be encountered. Using mobile devices at work, connecting to the office network, connecting to the Wi-Fi at a friend's house, connecting at the local coffee shop, and so on, opens mobile devices to additional risks.

Figure 2.3 shows an example of how one can map their house.

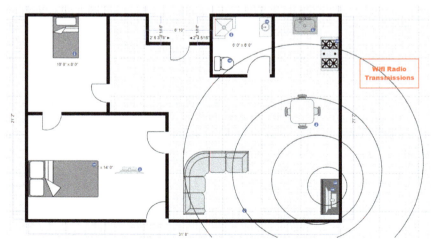

FIGURE 2.3 Mapping the house.

When mapping one's house, users should physically draw where their routers are. It's important to remember that the average stock home router broadcasts Wi-Fi signals approximately one hundred feet away. One can look at their router's manufacturer's Web site to determine how far it broadcasts.

SOME BLUETOOTH DANGERS

Bluetooth technology, while convenient and widely used, can pose some potential dangers if not secured properly. One of the main risks is eavesdropping, as Bluetooth signals can be intercepted by hackers who can gain access to sensitive information such as passwords, credit card numbers, and personal conversations. This can lead to identity theft, financial loss, and invasion of privacy. Additionally, unsecured Bluetooth connections can also be vulnerable to malware attacks, allowing hackers to take control of devices.

To secure Bluetooth and minimize these risks, there are a few precautions that users can take. First, it is important to keep Bluetooth turned off when not in use, as this will prevent unauthorized devices from connecting to your device. Only pair with trusted devices and avoid using Bluetooth in public places where hackers may have the opportunity to intercept your connection. Don't set devices to "discoverable" mode so devices cannot detect and connect to another device without permission.

Some other common Bluetooth threats can be pairing your phone to a rental car. The pairing can conveniently download your contact list, emails, and text messages. If you don't delete this information data from the rental car (or an old car you trade in) other people can potentially access your data.

WHO ELSE IS WATCHING YOUR WEBCAM?

You carefully set up that webcam to watch your house or your children while you were away. It has been great to see if your children made it home on time or if they are doing their homework after school. It's unnerving to think about who else might be watching your webcam? If you do not pay attention to your security on this neat new toy, anyone in the world could potentially be watching your kids all day and you at night. The Web site Shodan (*www.shodan.io*) provides white hat (ethical) hackers as well as criminals, sexual predators, and the government of any country the ability to find and identify unsecured webcams connected to the Internet. Finding devices on the Internet can be as simple as going to their Web site (*www.shodan.io*). Unsecured systems, cameras, printers, and other devices connected to the Internet can and are scanned for access. Your camera in your house, which you thought was plug-and-play easy, may be broadcasting your living room to the world. You can simply search for your IP address by going to the Shodan Web site and entering your

IP address. If Shodan has crawled the IP address any information, it will be found there.

Webcam Gate

In 2010, a Pennsylvania school district agreed to pay $610,000 to settle a federal lawsuit. The suit, which was dubbed the "Webcam Gate" scandal involved the school surreptitiously and remotely activating webcams embedded in school-issued laptops the students were using at home [Robbins 2010]. This is a cautionary tale to be aware of what devices are brought into your home and to act accordingly. This includes employer-owned devices you bring home that may have remote monitoring capabilities similar to that used by the school in this case.

TEXT MESSAGE SECURITY

Texting can pose a variety of dangers, one of them being the interception of SMS messages. This means that someone can access and read the contents of text messages without the phone owner's knowledge or consent. This can be particularly concerning when it comes to sensitive information such as bank account numbers or credit card details. Even simply sending a photo of a credit or debit card to a friend or relative can put one's financial security at risk if intercepted. Furthermore, the data remains on the service provider's network, making it vulnerable to hackers or other malicious actors. It is important for individuals to be cautious about the way they communicate, especially on their cell phones, and take steps to protect their personal information.

To avoid the dangers of SMS interception, it is crucial to be mindful of the information that is shared through text messages. These issues can be avoided by opting for more secure methods of communication such as encrypted messaging apps. The best practice would be to regularly review one's text message history and delete any messages containing sensitive information.

PROTECTING ONE'S VEHICLE

We all know that technology is increasing becoming a part of our vehicles from Bluetooth capability and GPS location to autonomous driving features. As we have previously stressed, security is not always a priority when these new features are implemented. These vulnerabilities allowed thieves to steal the vehicle with the use of a USB device or allow hackers to remotely control the vehicle such as starting or stopping it. The modern car owner must become acquainted with their vehicle's computer functions and as well of keeping up with all manufacturer's computer updates. An obviously important first step is to change the default passwords. Do Internet research on the vehicle and its computers for updates on known vulnerabilities and address them. For other steps check out the *Physics World* article titled "How to hack a self-driving car" [Ornes 2020].

CONCLUSION

Understanding the fundamental concepts of cybersecurity is essential in protecting individuals and their digital information in today's digital world. This chapter discussed the risk of connecting to the Internet and made suggestions for ranking those risks particularly as they relate to IoT devices. The key to mitigating those risks is the use of a properly configured router. The chapter also provided checklists for router configuration and for documenting the devices that connect to the Internet. Chapter 3 will go beyond the router and discuss additional measures that need to be in place for online cybersafety.

REFERENCES

Ornes, S. 2020. "How to hack a self-driving car." *Physics World,* August 18, 2020. *https://physicsworld.com/a/how-to-hack-a-self-driving-car/*

Robbins 2010. *Robbins v. Lower Merion School District, Dist. Court*, ED Pennsylvania 2010 Civil Action No. 10-665.

Whittaker, Z. 2017. "Security researcher says DirecTV hardware can be easily hacked." ZDNET, December 12, 2017. *https://www.zdnet.com/article/security-researcher-says-directv-hardware-can-be-easily-hacked/*

CHAPTER 3

SAFELY GOING ONLINE

IN THIS CHAPTER

Going online can expose users to risk. This chapter identifies those risks and covers steps to eliminate them. It specifically covers browsers, cookies, antivirus, antispyware, and firewall software, connecting via virtual privacy networks (VPN) and Wi-Fi. It also discusses the differences between privacy versus security.

INTERNET RISKS

Chapter 2 covered steps for securing home networks to ensure no one has access to the user's devices. Going online exposes users to other risks that must be addressed. This chapter explores other areas that must be addressed to ensure the users are secure while online. Keep in mind that the Internet is not just the World Wide Web, it includes every protocol that uses the Internet. This includes email, music-sharing tools, file sharing, and many other basic functions that are often taken for granted when accessing the Internet. All these many useful Internet tools can give bad actors access to user's computers.

Considerations for Securing the User's Computer for Online Use

Technology is always changing and so are the attacks against it. Online research can overwhelm the average person with conflicting advice as to what security means. The cybersecurity industry must evaluate the threat against the system to help determine what security measures to put into place. The average home computer or small business has different risks than a larger company. The following section evaluates the small office/home office (SOHO) risks posed by an Internet connecting computer.

Evaluating the Risk

Risk assessment is the process of evaluating and analyzing potential vulnerabilities and threats. It helps users determine the likelihood of a threat occurring and to identify potential consequences if those threats were to materialize. This process helps identify areas that need improvement and additional security measures that could be added to protect the home network. Table 3.1 covers this process.

TABLE 3.1 Risk Assessment

	Step	Evaluation
1.	Assets Identification	The first step is to identify all the assets in one's home network, such as computers, routers, connected devices, and personal data.
2.	Threat Assessment	Identify potential threats that could compromise the security of the network, such as malware, phishing attacks, physical theft, or human error.
3.	Vulnerability Assessment	Identify any vulnerabilities or weaknesses in the network that could make it more susceptible to attacks, such as outdated software, weak passwords, or unsecured Wi-Fi networks.
4.	Risk Analysis	Evaluate the likelihood and potential impact of each identified threat, taking into account the user's network's vulnerabilities.
5.	Prioritization	Prioritize the risks based on their potential impact and likelihood of occurrence. This will help the user focus on the most critical risks first.
6.	Risk Mitigation	Develop a plan to mitigate or reduce the identified risks. This may include implementing security measures such as installing antivirus software, enabling firewalls, updating software, and using strong passwords.
7.	Implementation and Monitoring	Implement the risk mitigation plan and regularly monitor the network for any new vulnerabilities or threats.
8.	Review and Update	Periodically review the risk assessment and update it as needed. Remember new threats and vulnerabilities are constantly emerging.

With these steps a SOHO computer user can identify and hopefully address potential risks to their network. Over the long run this makes the network more secure and less susceptible to attacks. The process is important, but it is never finished. Regular review and updating the risk assessment helps to ensure the ongoing security of the user's network.

BASIC SOHO COMPUTER SECURITY CONSIDERATIONS

Thus far, the chapter has looked at the risk and tried to evaluate the kinds of things needed to address network threats. What are some of the things the user can actually do to affect network security? The following list explores some of the basics:

1. *Install a SOHO Firewall*
A local firewall is a great place to aid in the identification of and prevention of outside network attacks. Numerous companies make a variety of devices that can aid in securing a home network. Having one in between the user's network and the Internet is a basic requirement for SOHO security.

2. *Configure/Update the Operating System*
   Does the user have a thorough knowledge of their operating system or just a general familiarity of its functionality? Windows users have different configuration concerns than Apple users. Linux users also have very different considerations than either of those two. Users need to review the security requirements and implement the best overall practices for their operating system.

3. *Antivirus/Spyware Detection Software*
   Modern systems are under attack from numerous external (and even internal) sources. The next step in the protection of a user's computer systems is to ensure that the computers have antivirus and spyware detection tools installed. This, again, is a complex area requiring some research, but it is a security necessity.

4. *Use a Virtual Private Networks (VPN)*
   VPN's can serve an important purpose in security. If the user's risk assessment determines that their browsing traffic can possibly be compromised, installing and using a VPN might be appropriate.

5. *Block Browser Cookies/Active Content*
   Cookies and other browser-tracking devices are used by marketing firms and Web site owners every day for legitimate purposes. They can be a privacy and security issue for users with an evaluated risk. Blocking and preventing the tracking of online behavior may be an effective strategy based on the user's potential threats.

6. *Install/Update Browser(s)*
   Browsers can be a complicated issue. There are many different browsers, and each has its strengths and weaknesses. Users should select a browser to match their risk profile and ensure it is current.

7. *Use Encryption*
   Encryption is something of a mystery to many users. The choice of when to use encryption is really based on their threat analysis. The average user is probably not going to need to use encryption. But the threat level determined in a user's evaluation will dictate those requirements. Keep in mind that the successful use of encryption depends on many factors. Is the data at rest (stored on a hard drive) or being sent in an email communication? Each has different requirements and impacts the effectiveness of encryption's use.

8. *Use a Secured Computer*
   A secure computer is one that user has identified the risk to it and then accomplished the steps necessary to positively secure that same device.

9. *Maintain Updates*

Keeping a device secure is a continual process. Once the system is secured, based on the technology and understanding at the moment doesn't mean it will be secured next month or even tomorrow. Keeping the operating system, the router, browsers, and the other software current is a critical and ongoing function. Figure 3.1 gives you a visual outline of the considerations listed above when setting up a computer for your home use.

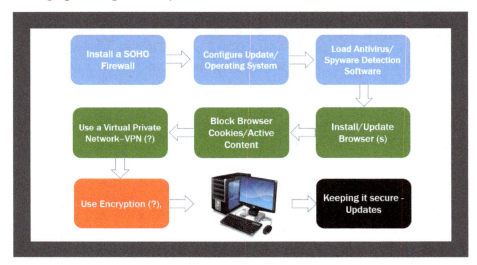

FIGURE 3.1 Considerations when setting up a computer.

EVALUATING THE USER'S INTERNET RISK

In today's digital age the Internet has become an integral part of everyone's daily lives. People use it for everything from connecting with friends and family to shopping and banking. The convenience and accessibility that the Internet provides comes with risks. It is important for users to evaluate those risks and take necessary precautions to protect their personal information.

The risks can include data posted online from various data breaches, online scams of which there are many, and the traditional threat of identity theft. It is essential to be aware of potential threats and be cautious when sharing personal information online. This can include using secure and trusted Web sites, regularly changing passwords, and being mindful of what information is being shared on social media. It is also important to be aware of who has access to personal data, including search engines and data aggregators. By evaluating risks and taking proactive measures, a user can better protect their personal information and enjoy a safer online experience. Once the user has risk awareness, they can take steps to minimize the threats. This can include the basics of using strong and unique passwords, being cautious of what information they share online, and regularly monitoring their accounts for any suspicious activity. It is also important to stay updated on security measures and potential threats by keeping informed on online safety practices. By evaluating Internet risks, the user can better protect themselves and their personal information while using the vast resources and connections that the Internet provides.

Going on the Internet is not just using the World Wide Web. Being on the Internet exposes users to various risks. It is important to be aware of these risks and take precautionary measures to protect personal information. One main risk is the data collected by search engines. Search engines store a user's search history and personal information. This data is sold and used for targeted advertising. The data sold to third parties is often done without a user's knowledge or consent. These data aggregators collect and sell personal and company data to various other companies. The data is used to define a user's buying behavior and makes it easier for data collectors to track their online activities. Moreover, hackers and other technology thieves pose a significant threat as they gain illegal access to a user's sensitive data through phishing scams, malware, or by exploiting vulnerabilities in user's devices and the systems storing their data.

THE OTHER RISKS A USER NEEDS TO KNOW

There is a whole slew of risks users may not have known about. They are also threats to user's personal information that they have little control over. These include a user's doctors, government agencies, and businesses they shop with online or in person. Many users don't even know as they are online associates with companies like eBay, Amazon, or Walmart.

Steps to Protect Personal Information (PI)

In today's world, there is nothing a user can do to guarantee protection of their personal data, but there are steps that can be taken to help prevent its misuse. Here are some of the steps users need to consider.

1. *At home/office.* We throw away a lot of material that has PI on it. One's garbage is full of it. Old-school hackers frequently used "dumpster diving" to locate PI and other sensitive information for later malicious use. Consider this when throwing away mail, pill bottles, and doctor instructions. Just like one does with recycling,

consider making a separate destruction box for these things that need to be securely destroyed by shredding, tearing up, or burning if permitted in one's community. Consider hiring a service to securely destroy items that contain PI.

2. *Two-Factor and multifactor authentication.* This adds an extra layer of security to a user's accounts by requiring a code or token in addition to their password. This can help prevent unauthorized access to accounts, even if someone has obtained the user's password. Smart phones also use authenticator apps. These are used to generate a one-time use code that is only known by the app and the Web site being accessed. Figure 3.4 describes how the basics of two-factor authentication works.

3. *Avoid using public Wi-Fi for sensitive activities.* Public Wi-Fi networks are often unsecure, making it easy for hackers to intercept a user's data. Avoid using public Wi-Fi for activities that require a user to enter sensitive information, such as online banking or shopping. This is of course unless a user has employed a VPN as previously described.

4. *Be wary of suspicious emails and messages.* Phishing scams are one of the most common methods used by hackers to obtain personal information. Be cautious of emails and messages asking for personal information or directing a user to click on suspicious links or open a document that wasn't requested. When in doubt, contact the sender or company using verified contact information (not the information provided in the message) to insure it is a legitimate request. A user can also look at the sender's email address to see if it is legitimate.

5. *Users should regularly monitor their accounts and credit.* Make it a habit to regularly check bank and credit card statements for any unauthorized charges. A user can also check their credit report for any suspicious activity. If a user notices any discrepancies, they should report them immediately. Opening accounts with the credit reporting agencies can also be a good tool for observing when changes to accounts are made. If one is concerned about their personal information being used to open new accounts, they can consider freezing their credit. This will prevent anyone from opening new credit accounts in a user's name.

6. *Users should use privacy settings on social media.* Social media platforms have privacy settings that allow users to control who can see their posts and personal information. It is important to review and adjust these settings to one's comfort level. Having accounts open to everyone on the Internet may not be the best option for one's personal security level. Users should periodically check these settings to ensure they remain accurate.

It is a common practice in the digital age for social media companies, data aggregators, and cell phone makers to collect information on user's every online move. Many companies use data tracking and analytics to better understand their audience and deliver more targeted advertisements. To protect one's information from these companies, a user can use ad blockers and limit the amount of personal information they share online. One can also review and adjust their privacy settings on various Web sites and apps. Additionally, being mindful of what one clicks on and which Web sites are visited also helps reduce the amount of data collected.

It is also a good idea to regularly review and delete apps and accounts one no longer uses to minimize their digital footprint. Users should stay informed about data breaches and take steps to protect their information if data is compromised. Overall, being mindful and cautious of one's online activity can go a long way to protecting personal information.

Privacy versus Security

Online security refers to measures taken to protect online information and systems from unauthorized access and potential threats. This includes implementing strong passwords, using firewalls and antivirus software, and frequently updating software and systems to prevent hackers from gaining access. Online security aims to ensure the confidentiality, integrity, and availability of online data and services.

Alternatively, online privacy refers to the control individuals have over the collection, use, and sharing of their personal information online. This includes keeping personal information such as name, address, and financial details private and not sharing it with third parties without consent. Online privacy also involves being able to browse, communicate, and conduct transactions online without fear of being monitored or having personal information collected without permission. While online security focuses on protecting data from external threats, online privacy focuses on protecting personal information from being accessed or used without permission.

BROWSER FUNCTIONS

Going on the Internet is not just using the World Wide Web. There is a whole process underlying typing a uniform address locator (URL) or address in a browser (or clicking on a link in Google or another search engine). The technical aspect is written in numerous books. There is a lot that goes on behind the scenes for one to get to their favorite Web site on the Internet. From a security point of view, users have to know what a browser tells other people and Web sites about them. Only with this knowledge can they hope to limit their risk exposure.

Selecting a Browser

It is important to consider which browser has the strongest and most reliable security features. Some popular browsers, such as Google Chrome and Mozilla Firefox, offer built-in protection against malware and phishing attempts. It is also important to keep one's browser up to date with the latest security updates and patches to ensure maximum protection. Additionally, look for a browser that allows for customization of security settings, such as adjusting the level of privacy and blocking certain types of cookies.

Select browsers that have a strong track record of protecting user data and respecting privacy rights. Browsers that offer features like private browsing or incognito mode can also add an extra layer of security by not storing your browsing history, cookies, or login information. Additionally, consider browsers that offer features like ad blockers or antitracking technology, as these can also help protect a user's online security and privacy. Ultimately, it is important to carefully research and compare different browsers to determine which one offers the best security features for a user's specific needs and concerns.

INITIAL BROWSER SET-UP

Some considerations when one downloads and installs a new browser can include blocking cookies. This is different in every browser. But this is a must to prevent Web sites from tracking who you are. Each browser handles blocking cookies in a different manner.

For a Chrome browser click the three dots icon in the top-right corner of the user's screen. This will open a popup screen. Click on *Settings*. The new tab reflected in Figure 3.2 will give the user access to *Privacy and Security* settings. For a user to locate how to access their particular browser's security settings, they should do a Google search with the following search parameters: browser privacy and security settings + (user's specific browser).

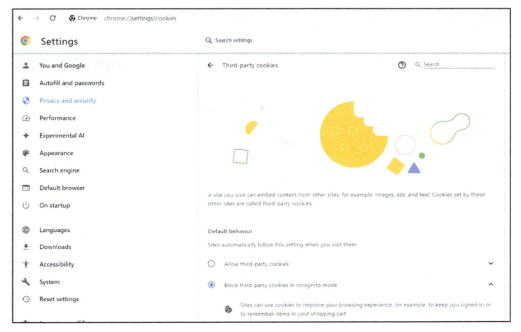

FIGURE 3.2 Chrome browser "privacy and security" settings.

ONGOING BROWSER MAINTENANCE

From time to time, one needs to clean out the clutter and remove cookies, browsing history, and temporary Internet files. One can use a tool that enables them to remove tracking devices from their systems such as CCleaner, Bit Bleach (made famous by its use to Hillary Clinton's system). This can also be accomplished under one's browser settings. Under one's browser's *Privacy and Security* section there are multiple options for protecting oneself. The default setting *Allow sites to save and read cookie data (recommended)* is on by default. From a security standpoint, this is not the most effective option for a user because it does not stop companies or bad actors from tracking their browsing. The best option is to select the *Block third party cookies*, however, the user must understand some Web sites won't appear properly if this is selected. The question is does the user want security or a great Web site experience? It's the user's choice, or chance, at being safe or allowing a bad actor the chance to access their system. Figure 3.3 describes how a browser communicates with a website to bring to your browser data and produce a website on your computer.

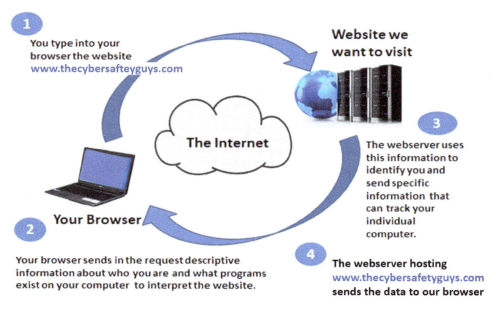

FIGURE 3.3 Web browser and server communication.

Two-Factor Authentication (2FA)

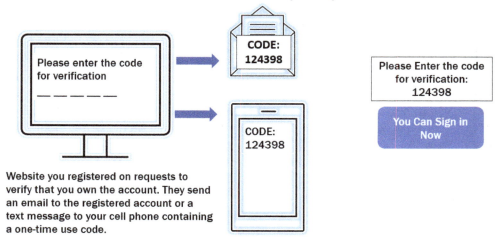

FIGURE 3.4 Two-factor authentication.

There are also many software applications too for blocking cookies and Web sites that are available for download. Some are included as browser extensions but depend on the browser you are using. There are many different types of ad blocking software's such as ADBlock or Ghostery that you might want to investigate to aid in your protection.

Additional Hiding Measures

A simple way to hide from data-seeking companies is to make up false identities. This is legal, but it might be a violation of the terms of a Web site's service. As long as one is not doing something that is illegal, the use of "sock puppet" (a false online identity) is common on the Internet. This is an extreme measure and takes a lot of effort to ensure that one is using false information regularly. The problem can be when the user wants to use their real identity to buy something on Amazon. Their browser might reveal the user's true identity.

In Private Mode

Private mode in a browser is a feature that allows users to browse the Internet without leaving any trace of online activity on the local device. This means that when using private mode, the browser will not save any browsing history, cookies, or temporary files on the user's device. This makes it a great tool for those who are concerned about their online privacy or for those who share devices with others. *Incognito mode* is what the Chrome browser calls private browsing. Also, keep in mind that using the private browsing mode won't protect one from online threats like phishing scams or other malware. It is also not an anonymous browsing tool. The user's Internet protocol address can be revealed to a Web site when visiting it even using the so-called private mode.

USING SOMEONE ELSE'S WIFI

Chapter 2 discussed routers and WiFi and the considerations for securing one's home network. What about when one is away from their home and using some other WiFi? How does one know that they are secure and what can be done about it? Accessing WiFi at a friend's house, the local coffee shop, or some other local business can put a user at risk. The user doesn't know what efforts they have taken to protect their network or who else may be spying on their network. One needs to protect their device before deciding to use these unknown WiFi networks. Here are some considerations:

1. Ensure firewall software is enabled prior to accessing the unknown WiFi.

2. Know the name of the public WiFi connection is correct. Ask an employee to be sure. Don't just assume the WiFi connection one sees is the correct one. Bad actors can set up similar names to trap users into accessing the wrong one.

3. Consider not using the WiFi connection if it does not ask for a username and a password. This is not secure. Some businesses will provide a common username and password to their regular customers. This is okay as it is not an open system with no security functions at all in place.

4. Prior to going out, turn off the function in your laptop or iPhone that automatically connects to the nearest WiFi connections. A user should do the same for Bluetooth connections.

5. Only connect to Web sites using the encrypted HTTPS service or SSL. This prevents one from possibly going to a site that may be malicious in nature. HTTPS ensures that communication to and from a particular Web site is secure. SSL is a form of encryption used by Web sites to secure communications.

6. Use a virtual private network or VPN (See VPN section). If using social -media accounts, ensure they have activated two factor authentication.

7. Turn off file and printer sharing and network discovery.

8. Turn off WiFi if it is not being used. This can prevent any accidental connection and attempts to access one's device when not at home.

KINDS OF WIFI ATTACKS

There are several types of WiFi attacks that a user may encounter. One common type is a man-in-the-middle attack (MITM), where an attacker intercepts and relays communication between the user and the wireless network. This allows the attacker to steal sensitive information such as login credentials or financial data. Another common attack, building on the MITM, is that a WiFi user may encounter a rogue access point or a fake WiFi hotspot mimicking a legitimate site. This is when an attacker sets up a fake wireless network in order to trick users into connecting to it. This allows the attacker to monitor and intercept the user's internet traffic like the MITM but control all the traffic. It is important for WiFi users to be aware of these types of attacks and take precautions to protect themselves and their data.

Identifying a WiFi Attack

The main way a WiFi user can identify a MITM attack is by paying attention to the network they are connected to. If the user notices they are suddenly connected to a different network without their knowledge, it could be a sign of a MITM. Additionally, the user may notice that their Internet connection is slower than usual or that they are experiencing frequent disconnections. This could be a result of the hacker intercepting and relaying the user's network traffic through their own router.

Another way to identify a MITM is to look for any suspicious activity on the network, such as frequent network interruptions or slow internet speeds. This could be a sign of someone intercepting and redirecting the network traffic. Additionally, checking the security certificate of the Web site one is trying to access can also help identify a man-in-the-middle attack. If the certificate is not valid or has been changed, it is likely that someone is trying to intercept the connection. It is important to always be vigilant and regularly check the network and device settings to stay protected from such attacks. It is also important for the user to be wary of any pop-up messages or alerts asking for personal information or login credentials, as these could also be a tactic used in a MITM. If the user notices any strange or unexpected behavior on their network, it is important to disconnect and investigate further to protect against potential attacks.

USING A VIRTUAL PRIVATE NETWORK (VPN) FOR BETTER SECURITY

A VPN is a secure connection to another network over the Internet. It allows one to communicate through the Internet without bad actors or governments viewing your traffic. It can also be used to access region-restricted Web sites or hide browsing activity from snooping bad actors when on an open or publicly accessible Wi-Fi connection. A VPN connects the user's device to another server somewhere on the Internet, which then allows one to browse the Internet using that computer's Internet connection. The rest of the world then sees this computer and not the user. It acts as a proxy preventing anyone looking for the users from identifying their real location.

How a VPN Works

The users connect their device to a VPN using software from that company. The user's device then acts as if it's on the same local network as the VPN. The user's browsing is then sent over an encrypted connection to the VPN service. One can connect to the Internet as if they were present at the VPN's location. The benefits of using a VPN on a public Wi-Fi is that users can now not be observed locally and cannot have their traffic intercepted. Keep in mind the use of a VPN only hides the user's traffic from observers. The VPN service sees all of the user's traffic. Figure 3.5 describes how a VPN works.

Basic Description of a VPN

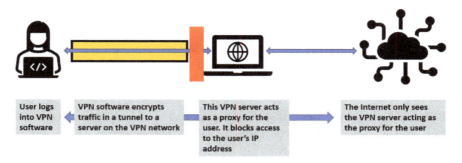

| User logs into VPN software | VPN software encrypts traffic in a tunnel to a server on the VPN network | This VPN server acts as a proxy for the user. It blocks access to the user's IP address | The Internet only sees the VPN server acting as the proxy for the user |

FIGURE 3.5 Basic VPN description.

Obtaining a VPN

The simplest way to find a VPN service is to do a simple search on a search engine for current VPN's. There are numerous VPN services available. Each and every VPN service has variation in its services and pricing. A little research will provide a list of compatible services for the user's needs.

Selecting the appropriate virtual private network (VPN) service can be overwhelming for novice Internet users. The first step in selecting the right VPN service is to understand one's needs. Identify why a VPN is needed and what features are essential for the user. For instance, if the user wants to access geo-restricted content, then look for a VPN with a wide server network. If the user wants to protect their online privacy, then look for a VPN with a strict no-logs policy. Knowing one's needs will help narrow down the options and make the selection process easier.

Next, research and compare different VPN services. Look for reviews and ratings from reputable sources and read through user experiences. Pay attention to factors such as speed, security protocols, user-friendliness, and customer support. Additionally, check the pricing plans and choose one that fits the budget. Some VPN services offer free trials or money-back guarantees, which can be helpful for novice users to test the service before committing to a long-term subscription. By doing thorough research and comparing different options, novice Internet users can select a VPN service that meets their specific needs and budget.

The most important factor for consideration is the level of security and privacy the VPN service offers. Novice Internet users may not be familiar with the various encryption protocols used by VPNs, so it is important to choose a service that offers strong encryption and follows industry standards for security. Additionally, some VPN providers keep logs of user activity, while others have a strict no-logging policy. For novice users, it may be best to choose a no-logging VPN to ensure maximum privacy. Users may also want to consider the VPN server locations and speed of the VPN service. These can impact browsing and streaming speeds for users. A user can also run the Web site URL through Google's Safe Browsing technology (*https://transparencyreport.google.com/safe-browsing/search?hl=en*) to see if the Web site has been flagged.

A USER'S PERSONAL DATA IS OUT THERE ALREADY

One of the things we often misunderstand about the Internet is the amount of data that is collected on various Web sites about us and our families. The simplest way to reveal how much data is possibly online about oneself is to Google your name. The data found may be a small amount of what actually exists in the databases of companies that collect data about oneself. The data collected about a user that is available on the Internet is collected from numerous places. For an even scarier experience about what personal data is online, go to a site like *www.spokeo.com*, *www.pipl.com*, or *www.zabasearch.com* and search your name.

Companies often referred to as *data aggregators* collect and sort our personal information to sell to others and for marketing purposes. If you are willing to pay a few dollars, these data aggregators will give you even more information. These data aggregators are companies that collect your data, try to clean it up and match it to your other data and then sell or distribute that information to other data publishers and marketers. Additional users of this data can include search engines, review sites, and your social media sites.

Removing One's Data from Data Aggregators

Data aggregators are Web sites that collect and store vast amounts of personal information from various sources such as social media, public records, and other online platforms. This data can then be sold to marketing companies, advertisers, or other interested parties. If one is concerned about their privacy and wants to remove their data from these aggregators, here are the steps you can follow.

First, identify the data aggregators that have one's information. The user can do this by conducting a simple online search or using a search engine. Once the aggregators have been identified visit their Web sites and look for their opt-out or removal policies. Some aggregators have a dedicated opt-out form that the user has to fill out, while others may require the user to email them directly. Make sure to follow the instructions carefully and provide all the necessary information to successfully remove your data. It is also a good idea to keep track of the aggregators one has opted out of for future reference. The user may also consider using online privacy protection services that can help them identify and remove their data from multiple aggregators at once.

The user can also go to Web sites like *https://www.privacyrights.org/data-brokers* and find access to additional information about these sites and how to remove their data from individual sites.

How Do Criminals Share User's Data?

This is a little more complicated and it would take another book to describe this properly. The bad actors are pretty good at using technology against us. They are using tools that hide who they are (referred to as anonymization) and places on the Internet that inhibits law enforcement's efforts to find them. These places are often referred to as the *Dark Web* or the *Dark Net*. This is not describing one place or one tool. There are multiple tools or browsers used to access hidden spaces on the Internet. In these anonymized Internet locations these bad actors openly share and sell stolen information about each of us. This can be email and passwords, or our credit card information. Any personal identifying information is available on these *Dark Markets*.

The most common of these is a tool called Tor. It can be found legitimately on the regular internet at www.torproject.org. It a registered nonprofit organization in the United States and is funded through donations (even from the US government). The Internet anonymization tool is used for legitimate purposes although the criminals have found it as their tool of choice for hiding from law enforcement. Keep in mind, depending on the user's evaluation of their personal online risk and security assessment, the Tor browser may be a tool that might fit one's security needs.

USING ANTIVIRUS OR MALWARE PREVENTION

Users need to think about how to stop bad elements from accessing their devices. Every time one goes on the Internet, someone unknown to them is trying to access their computer, give them some code the user doesn't want, and manipulate the user's online experience. The reality is marketers often engage in some of this activity legally. There are plenty of bad guys trying to steal the user's information too. The following section takes a look at the kinds of software the user should have on their systems prior to venturing out onto the Internet. This is an agnostic look at the software features and not a brand name review.

Antivirus/Malware Detection Software

There are numerous manufacturers of antivirus and malware detection software. Some are offered for free, and some require payment. What are the best practices these types of software should provide for its customer? When selecting antivirus/malware detection software, it is important to consider the features and capabilities of each option. Look for software that offers real-time protection, meaning it can constantly scan and detect any threats as they happen. It should also have a strong detection rate for both known and unknown threats, as well as the ability to quarantine and remove any detected malware. Additionally, consider the software's user-friendliness and compatibility with your operating system. Good antivirus/malware detection software should come with features such as a firewall, email and Web protection, and automatic updates. These features can further enhance the overall security of the user's device and protect against a variety of cyberthreats. It is also important to choose software that offers customer support and has a good track record of promptly addressing any issues or vulnerabilities. Keep in mind that no software can guarantee complete protection against all malware types, so it is crucial to practice safe browsing habits and regularly backup important data as an additional layer of protection.

It's also important to choose a reputable and trusted brand, as well as regularly update the software to ensure it can keep up with the constantly evolving cyberthreat landscape. A great way to determine the best software for a user's purposes is to read reviews. One can then compare prices to determine the best value for their specific needs.

Antivirus/malware detection software can be memory intensive. Be sure to have a significant amount of RAM on your machine to adequately run the software and not affect the operation of the other software.

Firewall Software

Firewalls are another level of protection from a different source than the antivirus software. Access to the user's systems can come from connections that come into their network that are not necessarily blocked automatically. Firewalls can provide the home user with protection from these attacks. One's router will have certain settings to protect users from these attacks. Adding a software firewall adds additional levels of reporting and protection to a system.

IDENTIFYING MALICIOUS WEB SITES

Malicious Web sites are often how user's systems get infected. There are a few key things to look out for in identifying these Web sites. First, pay close attention to the Web site's URL. If it looks suspicious or unfamiliar, it's best to steer clear. Malicious Web sites often have unusual or misspelled URLs or may use numbers or symbols instead of words. Their URLs will often have subtle differences from legitimate Web sites. This is a common tactic used by scammers to make their Web sites look legitimate.

Another red flag is if the Web site asks for personal information or login credentials, especially if it's not a secure site (indicated by a padlock icon next to the URL). Ensure the Web site's URL starts with *https* instead of just *http*. Pay attention to the Web site's design and layout. If it looks unprofessional, cluttered, has excessive spelling or grammatical errors, or has a lot of pop-up ads, it could be a red flag for a fake or malicious site. If the Web site has a lot of pop-up ads or asks the user to download something unexpectedly, it's best to be cautious. These could potentially be tactics used by hackers to install malware on the user's device. Even declining the request can lead to an infection. When in doubt exit the site by closing the browser. It's also important to research the Web site before clicking any links or downloading anything. The user can do this by using a search engine to look up the Web site and see if there are any reports of it being a scam or malicious. Consider running the Web site URL through Google's Safe Browsing technology (*https://transparencyreport. google.com/safe-browsing/search?hl=en*) to see if the Web site has been flagged. By being vigilant and following these steps, one can prevent accidentally downloading malware or falling for phishing scams.

When a user receives a suspicious email or link directing them to a Web site, they should avoid clicking on it, and instead manually type in the Web site's URL to ensure they are accessing the legitimate site. Overall, being cautious and paying attention to these warning signs can help prevent unknowingly downloading malware or falling victim to a phishing scam.

To prevent the accidental download of malware or phishing, it's important to have strong security measures in place. This includes using reputable antivirus software and keeping it up to date. Additionally, the user can install a Web browser extension or plug-in that flags potentially malicious Web sites. It's also important to regularly back up important files and information in case one's device does become infected with malware. Last, one must trust their instincts and use caution when browsing the Internet. If a Web site or download seems suspicious, it's better to err on the side of caution and avoid it altogether. Remember, prevention is key in protecting oneself from malicious Web sites and potential cyberattacks. By being vigilant and following these steps, users can prevent accidentally downloading malware or falling for phishing scams.

OTHER CYBER RISKS

There is a whole slew of risks to users and their family that are not known. They are also threats to the user's personal information that they have little control over such as data collected at one's doctor's offices, government data collection, businesses users shop with, and even businesses they don't interact with that buy and sell data.

Perhaps the most obvious risk is the possibility of a data breach or hacking of personal data when stored by someone else (usually a business). With the increasing use of technology and online platforms, a user's personal information and data are more vulnerable than ever. A data breach can result in the theft of sensitive information such as social security numbers, credit card numbers, and even medical records. This can lead to identity theft, financial loss, and even blackmail (think ransomware).

Another risk that may not be immediately apparent is the potential for one's personal information to be sold or shared without consent. Companies and businesses often collect vast amounts of data on their customers without their knowledge, and this information can be sold to third parties for various purposes. One might consider this a violation of your privacy, and it does put the user at risk for targeted advertising, fraud, and other malicious activities. One signs terms of service without reading them. Users unfortunately often create these problems. It is important to be cautious and aware of how one's information is being collected, used, and shared, and to take steps to protect one's privacy as much as possible.

THE MEDIA COMPANIES WHO COLLECT USER'S EVERY ONLINE MOVE

Media companies have become a crucial part of our daily lives as they are responsible for providing us with news, information, and entertainment. Many of these companies are also collecting our every move online. These media companies are often referred to as the *big players* in the digital world, and they include major platforms such as Google, Facebook, Amazon, and Twitter. They use sophisticated algorithms and tracking technologies to gather data on a user's browsing habits, social media interactions, and online purchases. This information is then used for targeted advertising and to create detailed profiles of a user's preferences, behaviors, and interests.

These media companies have a vast reach and influence, with billions of users across the globe. They have access to an immense amount of personal data, and their constant monitoring of our online activities raises concerns about privacy and security. While they claim to use this data for personalized user experience and to improve their services, the lack of transparency and control over how our information is being used is a growing concern. As these companies continue to expand and dominate the digital landscape, it is important for consumers to be aware of the extent of their data collection and take steps to protect their privacy.

The constant collection and tracking of personal data by media companies has raised concerns about privacy and security. Many users are unaware that their every move online is being monitored and their information is being sold to third parties. This has led to debates about the ethical implications of such practices and calls for more transparency and regulation in the industry. While media companies argue that this data collection is necessary for providing personalized and relevant content to users, critics argue that it is a violation of privacy rights. As technology continues to advance, the role and impact of media companies in collecting and using personal data will continue to be a topic of discussion and concern.

Personal Risk Assessment

Considering all the topics discussed in this chapter you can begin to assess the possible threats to your personal home network and family. In Table 3.2 Risk Assessment, we have provided a list of considerations that you can use to guide your personal identification of the weaknesses in your home use of technology. Use this list as a basic guide and add additional items that might be unique to your personal home environment. As you complete the checklist make a note of when you reviewed this and how you accomplished it.

TABLE 3.2 Risk Reassessment

Things to consider	Reviewed/completed
Uset strong and unique passwords for all online accounts.	
Avoid using default passwords for devices and change them regularly.	
Avoid using easily identifiable information, such as your full name or birthdate, in online usernames or passwords.	
Use a password manager to securely store and generate strong passwords for all accounts.	
Enable two-factor multifactor authentication for added security. Use an authenticator app when available.	
Regularly update software and operating systems to protect against security vulnerabilities.	
Use reputable antivirus software and keep it updated.	
Use a firewall to protect against unauthorized access to your computer or network.	
Use a secure browser and enable the Do Not Track feature to prevent Web sites from tracking your online activity.	
Read and understand the privacy policies of Web sites and apps before providing personal information.	
Identify the privacy settings on social media and adjust them for one's security needs.	

Things to consider	Reviewed/completed
Be cautious of phishing emails and never click on suspicious links.	
Don't share personal information on social media platforms or in online forms or accounts.	
Avoid using public Wi-Fi when possible.	
Use a virtual private network (VPN) when accessing the internet on public networks.	
Regularly back up important data on external hard drives or secure cloud storage.	
Use a shredder for sensitive documents before disposing of them.	
Keep personal devices, such as laptops and smartphones, physically secure and use passcodes or biometric authentication to prevent unauthorized access. Don't leave devices unattended in public places.	
Avoid using public computers or shared devices for sensitive tasks such as online banking or shopping.	
Regularly review bank and credit card statements for any unauthorized charges or suspicious activity.	
Educate yourself on current security threats and stay vigilant in protecting your personal data.	

CONCLUSION

Going on the Internet is not without security issues. This chapter covered the best security practices for a variety of tools and features available. Chapter 4 discusses additional steps to secure social media.

Chapter 4

Securing Social Media

IN THIS CHAPTER

This chapter covers securing social media. It discusses the concerns and risks of social media use and the approaches to secure one's personal data online. This includes password security and how important maintaining secure passwords is in an online world.

SOCIAL MEDIA USE

Social media is as ubiquitous as the telephone and television. Increasing it is used not only to connect to friends and family but also as a necessary business tool. Unfortunately, social media security is an afterthought for most users. We live in an environment where many social media accounts have been broken into and no one is immune. It is a digital survival necessity that one considers what social media security means and implements its requirements.

Many argue the best thing to do to protect oneself from any security issues is to simply never open any social media accounts in the first place, and if the user did, they should immediately close and delete them. This is the equivalent of becoming a modern-day hermit. This is not a realistic approach in today's world as access to not only individuals, but goods, services, and information is greatly enhanced through social media connectively. Account break-ins are unfortunately becoming more common. In September of 2018, an attacker obtained digital credentials that allowed them to access Facebook users' information, including names, birth dates, current cities, hometowns, and more, which affected an estimated twenty-nine million people. These massive breaches against a provider make headlines, but they are not the only attacks happening. Individuals are often singled out or targeted by attackers looking for information that can be used to extort or embarrass users or to gain access to other accounts of value, such as a bank account. This chapter will discuss how to secure a user's social media accounts to minimize the risk, whether it comes in the form of a massive breach or a targeted attack. Hopefully, during the process, the user will become aware that what one posts on social media has a long shelf life and may someday be viewed by individuals beyond their intended audience.

Social media entities do not provide their services as philanthropic gestures to the public. They use their platforms to make money. They drive content to users' feeds based on their proprietary algorithm. These formulas scrutinize surfing habits, likes/dislikes, posts, online shopping, contacts, geolocation, and a host of other unknown criteria to drive content to users. Companies pay social media to use this information to sell goods and services to users. All of this is done to make users addicted to social media and the goods and services being pushed on this twenty-first-century platform.

Businesses aren't the only ones trying to use social media to change thoughts and behavior. As was seen during the 2016 US elections countries are willing to use social media to manipulate the actions of users, including how individuals vote. It is important to discuss these issues to reduce one's risk of being manipulated.

THE VALUE OF USER'S INFORMATION TO OTHERS

Information is valuable for both legitimate and illegitimate reasons. Family, friends, coworkers, and business partners can have a legitimate reason for knowing personal information. Criminals can use our personal information to cause both financial and physical harm to us and our loved ones. The following list describes the value of personal information:

1. *Mining Personal Information*: Publicly open social media accounts provide leads to a user's interests, family, and friends. These leads identify where one shops, lives, and goes to school. It could potentially provide information on a user's banking and investing account locations. This information can be used as a real-world attack. It could be used to create a password dictionary to help in a brute force attack on social media accounts, emails, and so on. Information gained can be used to trick users or others in a social engineering act to gain access to an account or system or trick one to send/authorize funds be transmitted.

2. *Gain Access to Work Accounts:* Information on social media can point to an employer's network, such as a work email, which can be used to attack that network. Users should make sure their social media does not link to their work email.

3. *Steal Users' Identity:* The theft of a single account can potentially lead to the access of other accounts the user has control over. It could also be used to register accounts on other sites.

4. *Blackmail:* Some strange people will get a user's sensitive or personal data, such as photos, to try and use it against the user. Harassment can occur as well as blackmailing the user for money or incriminating photos. This has become an issue for teenagers chatting online with strangers.

5. *Impersonation:* An increasing concern is the taking of photos from a user's account to create a fictitious social media account to trick others into providing access to their accounts or to commit fraud.

REVENGE PORN

Unfortunately, some individuals have no issue with using the most intimidating images to get back at someone. People post unflattering nude images of other people on the Internet out of spite. Angry and emotional people do things that due to the Internet's nature cannot be undone. Electronic images do not degrade like paper images. They can easily be copied and disseminated from device to device. Once these images are posted online, they can literally spread worldwide. Once online they can be downloaded, copied, and even cached by search engines. One embarrassing image can become millions of exact copies. Regrettably, it's typically a former sexual partner trying to embarrass or harass someone. The image is posted without consent revealing nude or sexually explicit images or videos. This is a crime in many jurisdictions and should never be overlooked as an innocent prank. This is clearly one of the dangers teens face when they take images of themselves which at the time seemed innocent and fun. Many teen romances end and the potential for these images to go beyond their intended audience is very real. Warning our kids of this potential pitfall needs to be a top priority. Sharing explicit images of teenagers (under eighteen) has always been a crime. Most states now also have laws prohibiting the nonconsensual posting of adult images. In 2018, a woman was awarded $6.45 million dollars in a civil case where her copyrights were violated as the defendant had impersonated her online with intent to harm, stalked her, and intentionally inflicted emotional distress [Doe v. Elam 2014].

ADDRESSING SOCIAL MEDIA RISK: SECURITY VERSUS PRIVACY

The first step in addressing social media risk is to identify all of a user's accounts. Document each account's username/email and password using a password manager (see Table 4.1). Close accounts the user no longer uses if they serve no purpose, as this will eliminate the risk that the account can later be compromised. For the remaining accounts the user needs to consider two related but separate concepts, namely, security and privacy.

TABLE 4.1 *Documenting the User's Social Media Accounts*

Social media account	Add username and password to password manager	Email	Check app security settings	Check app privacy settings

Read the Fine Print

Users often sign on to the newest and brightest thing and social media accounts are no different. We frequently do not bother to read user agreements prior to signing up. We typically just hit the accept button and never read the contents. The same thing holds for social media privacy policies. Most people click through and don't actually read them. Users should take a moment to read the agreement before assenting to be bound by its conditions. One might be surprised by what they agree to. Also, users should read the privacy policy and what the social media site says about how they are going to use one's data. Many times, it's sold to other companies, or covered under the agreements as *sharing* your data.

Another security concern is how companies will handle account breaches. The user should understand what the social media site will do if their data is stolen from the site. The very companies that the user wants to do business with could be a real threat to their personal information. These agreements are important, but users should be aware that social media sites don't always aggressively look for violations. For instance, consider Facebook and Instagram, both of which are owned by Mega. Both prohibit sex offenders from using on their site. This does not mean that sex offenders aren't on their site. They frequently sign up with bogus names or even their real name and get on the sites. Neither Facebook nor Instagram are scouring sex offender registrations or doing criminal background checks to deactivate sex offender accounts. They rely on individual users to report these profiles to them. They are better with removing pornography and other prohibited content but make no mistake these things can still be found on their sites. This is just something to think about when allowing children on sites. There is still an element of risk that they might be exposed to something inappropriate even if prohibited by a social media agreement or policy.

The user has to make a decision after reading the social media site policy and agreement. Can the user adjust anything on their end, such as how they actually use their social media account, to make it still acceptable to maintain? If the user can't make personal adjustments, then they should deactivate the social media account. One should be able to deactivate it as they read the policy/agreement. Users should be aware that these agreements can be modified, and they should continue to evaluate if they are the right fit. Users are not bound to any social media for life.

Increasingly there are other agreements beyond those provided by social media that users all need to be aware of. Almost all employers have standalone policies or some provisions that deal with how their employees use social media. Employers are not alone. Schools from elementary through colleges also have such provisions. Even fraternal organizations and clubs will often have social media policies. Collectively these policies govern such things as who can create a social media presence for the organization, and what things can and cannot be posted by employees/students/members on social media. Even if there isn't a specific social media policy, organizations frequently take the view that something posted online that reflects unfavorably on an organization or its members can and will result in some kind of adverse action. The news is full of stories of employees or students whose online post or association with some social media group resulted in them getting disciplined or terminated by their organization as their conduct violated an explicit social media policy or implicit behavior policy.

SECURITY

Security is of paramount importance. If the user's social media account is not secured then an attacker can gain complete access, regardless of what privacy settings one may have selected. Every social media service has a different method of securing their users' access to the service. Many users simply make an account and login without thinking about what the service's security function includes. Most never look at the changeable features to identify the possible safer functions that could enhance security. The following are some of the types of security that should be available to the user to protect their accounts.

Contact Email/Cell Phone

A contact email is one required by most social media sites as a method to contact the accounts. In some cases, a social media account may request an additional email address as a backup in case the user's access to the original is lost. Make sure to provide a backup email address if permitted. Cell phone numbers are also asked for two-factor authentication purposes.

Passwords

The first step is to have a strong password. The password must not be easily guessed by someone who knows the user or by information users openly provides. For instance, if one is a diehard sports fan, who wears their favorite team's jersey all over the place and posts online team comments/updates, it would not be a good idea to use a password that is not associated in some way with their favorite team. One should also have a separate password for each social media account. Also consider periodically changing the passwords. Consider using a password manager to assist in creating and storing passwords. If there is ever a breach, immediately change the password, don't wait for a notice from the social media company to do it. Also change the password for the associated email accounts for that social media account. Finally, don't keep passwords near your devices.

Tips for Creating a Strong Password

A brute force attack occurs when a computer program is used to try passwords until it finds one that works. Such programs can be particularly effective if information is known about the user who created the password to be cracked. This information provides a *dictionary* of possible passwords to try first in the attack. Accounts as well as devices frequently are set to lock the account/device after so many failed attempts that minimize a brute force attack's success. To further guard against such attacks consider the following tips:

1. The longer your password the better. It should be between eight and fourteen characters in length. Use a mix of characters (numbers, uppercase and lowercase letters, and special characters, e.g., *, #, etc.).

2. Consider creating a passphrase instead of a password. A passphrase is a group of words, which can be easily remembered, for instance, the strong will survive. One can also use the phrase as a starting point and mix it up a bit by substituting numbers or special characters for letters and mixing in upper case letters. The above passphrase might become. The "Stron* will surv!ve", by using uppercase letters for the first two words and substituting the ! special character for the letter. Quotes can also be used as passphrases, provided they substitute characters for letters and include upper case letters.

3. Consider using a password or passphrase generator, which can be located online. Once the user has a password or passphrase, they can further modify it for use on each social media account. For instance, if your passphrase is *The Stron* will survive* apply "add FB" at end for the Facebook account, TW for Twitter, and so on for each social media account.

Password Managers

Password managers come in several flavors. The user can download one that is only on their local machine or use the ones that are resident in their browser. There are also ones that can be used across devices. There are generally commercial password managers that require an annual fee. The following list explores the pros and cons of each type.

1. *Downloaded password managers.*
    Downloaded password managers can be the safest because they are only on the user's computer. If a user has one that requires a password to access it, don't keep it open all the time in order to keep your passwords safe.

2. *Browser password managers.*
    Most modern browsers can store passwords in the browser for ease of use. This is popular and commonly used as a storage location. From a security point of view, these can be dangerous. If the browser is insecure the password can be compromised. Again, this is balancing security with ease of use.

3. *Cross platform password managers.*
    Many of the password managers offer the ability to use their systems to store passwords. The advantage is that a user can then access the passwords from their cell phone, a computer at work, or a tablet. This has obvious advantages and makes use of passwords across the user's many devices easier. From a security point of view, there are now multiple places that can expose the user's password. Selecting this as an option needs to be carefully considered by the user.

A definite security function should be to never allow automatic logins. Ensure cell phones, computers, or other devices are password protected so if someone finds them on, they can't login into the user's accounts through their browser.

Security Questions

Security questions are a commonly used feature on many Web sites for verification of a user when accessing a Web site. This feature requires the user to answer several questions. Unique answers are then required to verify the user's access. One or multiple questions can be asked to gain entry to a Web site. Be cognizant of the answers provided. For instance, if it asks for the users to name their first teacher, boss, and so on, consider a consistent method, such as always providing only the first name or full name for such questions. Otherwise, the user might not be allowed in if they provided the full name at initial setup, but later responded by just giving a first or last name when asked. The same thing applies for questions asking for the location of your first kiss, job, home, and so on. Did the user initially provide just the city, or did they provide the city and state? If they provided the state did they abbreviate it or spell it out? Implementing a standard practice will keep users from getting stumped by questions they obviously know the answers to.

Two-Factor Authentication

Once the user has their passwords selected, they need to set up two-factor authentication for each account. Two-factor authentication relies on a user to provide a password and one additional security feature to prove who they are when accessing a social media account. Most often this second feature involves a cell phone number. Once the individual provides a password a text message or call is initiated, providing a separate code to the identified number. This code then must be provided to the account to gain access. Be aware that if the user didn't password protect their cell phone and it is stolen, the thieves can defeat two-factor authentication protection as they will receive that text message or call providing the code. Scammers may perform SIM card swaps to deactivate your phone and gain control of your two-factor verfication codes. To prevent this, setup a PIN or password on your celluar accounts to protect against unauthorized changes.

Other security features, such as biometrics, can also be used. This would include fingerprints or facial scans. A scan must then be provided to gain access to the account. Beware that criminals have found that they can trick a user into proving a facial scan to them which can then later be used to defeat this security feature to access the user's account. There are also hardware-based security keys, such as USB drives for two-factor authentication. Using two security features provides a user with a higher level of assurance than authenticating account access with just a password.

Privacy

The next thing the user needs to do is to review the privacy settings with each account. Doing this will help to ensure that they have done the most to protect themselves online. Following are several things users can do when they are logged into each account to tighten up the privacy settings and prevent any wrongdoing with their accounts.

1. *Tighten up privacy settings.*

    a. Each social media service has different privacy settings. As a new user, and as a regular user, these settings need to be checked on a regular basis because social media companies change these settings and often don't tell users. One's privacy could not be as secure as possible if left unchecked.

2. *Turn off geotagging or location identification.*
    a. Geotagging occurs in so many functions now. One of the most obvious is the tagging of a user's photos with the geolocation they were taken. This can be dangerous and compromise one's safety. For example, if a child takes photos with the geotagging feature on and posts the photos online, they could potentially be providing a stalker with the exact location of their bedroom. Not all social media keeps this data when images are posted, but why risk this occurrence?
3. *Remove third-party plugins or apps.*
    a. Third-party plugins and apps may seem cool on a social media site. When used they are often leaving the social media site's security and going to an unknown site with questionable security. Taking that survey from Facebook about what kind of animal a user is could lead to allowing an unknown company in an unknown country access to one's phone.
    b. Review of social media profile. Sites such as Facebook and LinkedIn allow users to see their profile as others would. Use this feature to review what others are seeing to insure information is not being inadvertently leaked.

Table 4.2 Social Media Security/Privacy Checklist has been added to provide you with a checklist for reviewing your social media and privacy. Use this checklist as a personal guide to help secure your social media accounts.

TABLE 4.2 Social Media Security/Privacy Checklist

Item	Facebook	Instagram	Twitter	LinkedIn	Other
Create a unique password.					
Set up two-factor authentication.					
Do you have security questions/answers?					
Never allow automatic logins.					
Privacy Items					
Review the user's basic information that is public.					
Remove profile information that the user doesn't want public.					
Set account to least amount of review by other persons.					
Limit who can connect with the user.					
Turn off geotagging or location identification.					
Check the ad settings and limit the ads.					
Remove third-party apps and don't allow logins using apps.					

STEPS TO AVOIDING SOCIAL MEDIA SCAMS

1. Be selective when accepting friends, posting, and clicking.

2. Be selective with people the user doesn't know. Accepting all requests to connect with can be dangerous. If one doesn't know someone, do they really want to connect with them? Fake accounts are used to try and gain access to user's accounts or to their connections. One should be suspicious of recently created accounts, particularly if they are portraying someone very likely to have created an account much earlier. Some accounts one may even know, but criminals impersonate friends trying to gain access to the user's account and friends list. It is not uncommon to see a fake account attempt to connect with user when the real person is already a connection.

3. Think twice before clicking on a link.

4. Be careful where one checks in from. Is geolocation on and has the user just alerted a burglar they are not home?

5. Don't share personal information online.

6. Be mindful of phishing scams.

7. Don't use social credentials to sign into third-party sites.

8. Avoid quizzes and games that may give access to a user's profile and other personal information. These are often designed for the user to reveal details about themselves that can be used to obtain a password or overcome two-factor authentication questions.

9. Avoid the clickbait material posted. Often, it is a breaking celebrity death or some news about the latest photos stolen from a celebrity. These can and often are attempts at gaining access to a user's device through links that are malicious.

USING PSEUDONYMS ON SOCIAL MEDIA

It is certainly possible to use different pseudonyms for different social media services. Social media networks want users to feel safe and trust one another and using a pseudonym does not denote trust. Given the current environment of phony accounts set up to allow bots (computer code that tries to act like a human) to respond on social media it's easy to see why companies only want real people. They are using techniques like requiring a user's cell phone to verify accounts. Gone are the days when people could make up multiple accounts and not have them associated with themselves. (Hackers and law enforcement still get around some of these security efforts.) Separate accounts may be a good way to ensure your personal protection.

Be aware that using a pseudonym on a social media account may be prohibited by the site. It can be deleted without notification and the user will likely lose all data associated with that account. Additionally, spoofing (using) another individual's identity is never a clever idea and is illegal.

OTHER THINGS NOT TO DO ON SOCIAL MEDIA

It is not necessary to post certain information on the Internet. It should be common knowledge by now not to post birth dates, addresses, family contact information, school information, and racy photos, but what other information should not be put online? What things should our children or other family members refrain from putting online?

1. Remember pictures users share online are no longer controlled by the user.
2. Before posting something that involves another person, they should be asked if they mind it being posted to a social media account.
3. Users should not trust emails from people the they do not know.

People love to share information on social media. When they go on vacation and leave their homes unoccupied, it is wise to not be so open with information. The things the user should avoid on social media while on vacation are:

1. Posting specific travel plans, specifically about when, where, or how long the user will be on vacation. Post these travelogue photos when back at home.
2. If the user can't wait to post about the trip or post their favorite selfie, they should do it to a tight group of friends or family and *not post them publicly.*
3. The best idea is to take a computer break while on vacation, and consider forgetting about social media for the trip.

DOES SOCIAL MEDIA REVEAL LOCATION?

Most social media sites can display the user's physical location if they allow it. Location is data one's phone collects from the GPS system. In some cases, the user's computer can also reveal location information based on the Internet Protocol address the computer uses when the user goes online. To not allow this to occur, check the setting of the social media app to prevent this from occurring.

Photos taken can also contain potential GPS location data. Some, but not all social media sites remove this data when posted online. Save the hassle and change the settings in your phone to stop the phone's photo function from collecting this information.

BEING ON SOCIAL MEDIA WITHOUT A PROFILE

Individuals may decide not to have a social media presence. This does not mean they will not find themselves being posted to social media profiles. Friends, schools, and employers will post an individual's pictures to social media, often without seeking permission. These images can include not only the picture but also identifying information. Be aware of who is taking pictures and what they intend to do with those images. Some entities will honor a request not to post them or to block the individual's face out of the image.

SOCIAL MEDIA ON THE USER'S CELL PHONE

Cell phone social media apps have a tendency to leak data whether or not the user wants it to. When the user agrees to download the app, they click through the agreements to allow the app access to everything on the phone. By giving the app permission to access the user's phone, one potentially is allowing them access to their personal information. It may seem the best advice is to remove all the apps from one's phone. Removing all the apps from our phone may not be practical in today's world. Communication apps and social media apps are how the world communicates. So, what can we do on cell phones to protect ourselves? Many of the same protections we have mentioned before apply to cell phones. Make sure the apps do not reveal more information than the user wants them to about who they are and where they are.

1. *Enable privacy.*
   Make sure to review the privacy settings of their smartphone and the settings of any apps one downloads. Set the privacy settings as high as the user feels is needed for their situation.

2. *Only download apps from Google and Apple stores.*
   Only download third-party applications from your operating system's actual store. Androids use the Google store and iPhone users use the Apple store. This helps to ensure the application has been reviewed and won't be malware. Research the apps before downloading them. A simple Google search may tell the user more about the app than the advertisement on the app store.

3. *Be suspicious.*
   People on the Internet send weird stuff to phone users such as weird text messages from someone one doesn't know, weird emails, and weird phone calls. Always be suspicious and don't just believe people or messages one receives. If the user doesn't know who they are from, delete them.

4. *Use two-factor authentication.*
   Two-factor authentication should be turned on for every app one uses. If the app does not verify your connection to the app, be wary and consider not using the app.

5. *Get a good password manager.*
   Password managers on cell phones help to prevent our using the same password repeatedly. Several good ones exist. Do a little research and the user will find one that suits their needs.

6. *Close old accounts.*
   Don't keep old accounts open. It is a huge security risk.

7. *Use a VPN on public Wi-Fi.*
   Use a VPN on your phone, especially when you are away from your home Wi-Fi network.

8. *Be mindful of app permissions.*
   Apps ask for way too many permissions. Pay attention to what one allows. If the app asks for too much access, consider uninstalling the app.

DATING AND/OR HOOK-UP SITES

Dating sites such as Match.com and hook-up sites such as Tinder are very much social media in that they require the user to set up a profile from which to interact with others on a network platform. Dating site profiles also require an email account. Even the raciest of these sites also have user agreements, and privacy and security settings. They usually initially allow users to create profiles for free but gaining access to many of the sites' major features require a monthly subscription. (Facebook also has its own site, Facebook dating, which is free.) Many sites also allow users to buy additional services, such as special profile prominence, additional messaging capabilities, and/or the ability to buy digital gifts/tokens. One major difference with these sites, particularly the hook-up sites, is users tend to use pseudonyms. Another difference is the users' goal by using these sites is to move from the online world to the real world (a date and/or hook-up). Some of these sites are designed to only generate revenue through the online communication services they offer users and don't want users to meet offline. The fine print appearing on many of these sites is the acknowledgement that the site is purely for entertainment purposes and users have no intention of meeting in person.

Remember those western movie scenes where the saloon ladies were constantly being friendly to get the cowboys to buy them drinks to make money for the saloon? It is the same principle in operation digitally. The profile keeps the user's interest and instead of buying drinks they get the user to buy tokens and messages to continue to be able to engage with the profile. These particular profiles, which no doubt are run by the site and not real individuals, are just there to get users to buy digital goods. Often these profiles will have a small *heart* on the profile identifying them as users only interested in online activities, specifically chat.

One fraudster technique is to connect with a user on a dating site for a few days and then request they continue their communication outside the dating site's purview. They will suggest chat apps like WhatsApp, Telegram, Signal, Google Chat, Viper, and so on. Once fraudsters get them on the chat app they will make a pitch as to why they need money or encouraging the user to invest in some scheme. Getting the user to switch to an outside chat app insures they don't have to worry about the dating site deleting their profile for something they can see on their network and be proven to be shady. These outside apps also create other avenues for a user to fall victim to cybercrime.

One would think that sites which collect a fee would do a better job of policing who is on its site, for instance prohibiting sex offenders on the site. Match Group, which owns free dating apps, such as Tinder, OkCupid, Plenty of Fish, and other free dating apps were found not to be screening whether users were registered sex offenders. [Holmes 2019]. A 2020 House subcommittee was investigating Tinder and Bumble for allegedly allowing minors and sex offenders to use their services [Ortuay 2020]. One would also assume that paid sites would not try to trick it's own consumer base. The Federal Trade Commission (FTC) sued online dating service Match Group, Inc. alleging that the company used fake love interest advertisements to trick hundreds of thousands of consumers into purchasing paid subscriptions on Match.com. [Federal Trade Commission 2019] These risks are in addition to nefarious users on the platform that are trying to commit romance scams and other online fraud schemes.

There are also stories of robbers and murderers using such sites to find their next victims. We encourage readers to avoid using these sites. Despite the clear risks many individuals may find value in the services offered by those sites and will disregard our warning. With that in mind here are some suggestions:

1. Users should not use even a portion of their name on these sites. These sites frequently require the user to say where they are located. The location and the user's name can be used to locate their profile on other sites, such as Facebook, which can lead to the user's full identity. With the user's full identity, they may be able to locate their actual address.

2. Avoid allowing these sites to connect to other accounts, such as Facebook to upload pictures for your profile. These uploaded or shared images can further be used to connect the user's dating profile with their off-line persona.

3. Be critical of all the "likes" and "messages," particularly those coming from geographic locations not nearby or in the user's interest area. They are either individuals trying to scam the user or the sites *profiles* to keep one interested in using the service.

4. Be very suspicious of profile pictures. Many users will use images pulled from other Web sites as their profile pictures. The user can do a reverse search using either Google Image search or TinEye and possibly find where else the image appears. There are also pay sites that will search images, such as Social Catfish (*https://socialcatfish.com/*) or FaceCheckID (*https://facecheck.id/*) A person using someone else's picture is a red flag to refrain from having any contact with them.

5. Never forward bank or financial information to a profile. It is always a scam. They are not going to use the funds to travel to meet the user.

6. If one is going to risk any real-world meeting, know who the user is going to meet. Get as much real information on that person as possible. Use it to check sex offender registrations lists. If possible do online criminal background checks. Make sure the meeting is in a very public place. Do not provide a home or work address. Users should tell someone where the meeting location is and who they are meeting and what time the meeting will be over. They should have their cell phone charged and with them at all times. Doing all this will allow the authorities to at least start the search to locate the user if needed.

TIKTOK

TikTok is a social media app that permits users to create, watch, and share short-form videos. The videos can be seen on TikTok but also appear on other platforms. In 2023, the FBI and US Department of Justice launched an investigation into TikTok including allegations that the company spied on American journalists [Hansen 2023]. Congress also had hearings and in 2024 passed legislation banning it in the United States [Associated Press 2024]. This is not the end as there likely will be court challenges to the law.

The United States wants to ban the application for several reasons. The main reason is national security, as TikTok is a Chinese company and there is a concern that the Chinese government will compel the company to provide user data, including from citizens of other countries. The United States previously banned the TikTok application on federal employees' phones. States have banned its use on public sector employees' phones in thirty-two of fifty states. This is an example that the real possibility exists that no matter how secure a company maintains personal data, it could be compelled to provide that data to others, including governments. In the United States it requires a warrant based upon probable cause to access data maintained by an Internet service provider. Other countries have different standards. So, keep that in mind when choosing social media, apps, and what to share or post.

CONCLUSION

Social media has changed the world we live in today. From the computers we use to the smartphone we carry; social media is ever present in our lives. This chapter discussed how to safely use social media and secure the different social media tools available to us. The next chapter will cover how to protect children online.

The use of technology by children presents positive things and some very terrible things. The next chapter will provide guidance on how to protect children from the forces of evil presently targeting children through technology.

REFERENCES

Associated Press. 2024. "What a TikTok ban in the US could mean for you." *AP News*, April 24, 2024. *https://apnews.com/article/tiktok-divestment-ban-what-you-need-to-know-5e1ff786e89da10a1b799241ae025406*

Doe v. David K. Elam II, 2:14-cv-09788-PSG-SS (C.D. Cal. 2014).

Federal Trade Commission. "FTC sues owner of online dating service Match.com for using fake love interest ads to trick consumers into paying for a Match.com subscription." Federal Trade Commission, September 25, 2019. *https://www.ftc.gov/news-events/news/press-releases/2019/09/ftc-sues-owner-online-dating-service-matchcom-using-fake-love-interest-ads-trick-consumers-paying*

Hansen, C. 2023. "Justice Department investigation TikTok owner for spying on U.S. journalists: Reports." *US News*, March 17, 2023.

https://www.usnews.com/news/national-news/articles/2023-03-17/justice-department-investigation-tiktok-owner-for-spying-on-u-s-journalists-reports

Holmes, A. 2019. "Tinder says 'there are definitely registered sex offenders on our free products.'" *Business Insider*, December 2, 2019.

https://www.businessinsider.com/tinder-says-registered-sex-offenders-use-app-match-group-2019-12#:~:text=Tinder%2C%20OkCupid%2C%20Plenty%20of%20Fish,ProPublica%20and%20Columbia%20Journalism%20Investigations

Ortuay, B. 2020. "Dating apps face US inquiry over underage use, sex offenders." *AP News*, January 30, 2020. *https://apnews.com/article/a93a6e2b02b7f979efca92ea7266e9f2*

5

PROTECTING CHILDREN

IN THIS CHAPTER

This chapter discusses protecting children from the risks associated with using new technology. It covers approving devices and processes for managing cyber risk.

CHILDREN AND TECHNOLOGY

Very few children in the developed world grow up without a computing device. A few years ago, it was computers, but now it is often a smartphone. Due to COVID-19 quarantines many schools provided computers to students for home use. Social media is an important aspect of children's lives. They share their lives online in ways most adults can't fathom. Not too long ago, the high school rock star was the sports player who got their picture in the newspaper. Today, there are YouTube famous kids who are unknown to many of us old enough to vote, making thousands of dollars a month talking about themselves. Other young adults film themselves playing video games and have hundreds of thousands of online followers. Technology has changed adult lives, but children have grown alongside that technology. Adults have to spend some time learning technology and how it works. Parents need to identify technology that can assist children in developing into law-abiding citizens both online and in the real world. Parents must also instill in them how to use that technology in a manner that does not place them or others at risk.

Keeping children safe in the digital world, just like in the real world, requires a commitment to effectively communicate to them the risks. This volume can provide users with technological suggestions to manage cyber risk. No matter how much the user secures family's devices, one can't control their children's access to other devices. Schools may have adequate controls, but what about the local library? What about a friend's house? Do their friend's parents manage cyber risk in their homes? Are they secure from cyberdangers? The reality is no matter how secure one makes devices, a committed child, either on their own, with a friend's help or, worse, a predator, can obtain the knowledge to overcome the best-laid protections. We are reminded of an FBI Special Agent's story of how they installed monitoring software on their children's computers to keep them safe. Much to the agent's surprise, the enterprising child found a way to defeat it.

Sexual predators are not all met online but can be teachers, coaches, and so on. Sometimes, these predators either provide a burner phone or provide funds for the purchase of an unmonitored phone to overcome any parental oversight. There have been cases where sexual predators have instructed their minor victims to remove or destroy computer hard drives as the last step before their minor target leaves to meet them to further frustrate law enforcement efforts to locate them after they have been reported missing by their parents. The only way to truly protect your child is to instill appropriate cyberpractices in them.

INSTILLING BEST CYBERPRACTICES

A simple Google search can locate numerous resources covering cybersafe practices for parents to use. Some good sites are safekids.com, which is now affiliated with *ConnectSaftey.org*, and *commonsensemedia.org*. Besides great resources, these sites provide pledges that can be printed and signed. Safekids.com provides separate pledges for under ten, preteens/teens, cell phone use, and for parents. Collectively, these pledges are broad statements that all can understand about what is and is not allowed. They also collectively include statements that make it clear that timeframes for use and computer management will occur. For very young children, the user likely will have to focus on certain elements, such as time frames of use, and notice they will be monitored. As the user's child develops and obtains more digital freedom, one will also want to continue communicating with them about parental expectations as the child ventures into the cyberworld. The important thing is that the statements are a starting point for parents to build upon in managing their child's cyber risk.

IDENTIFYING NEEDS AND TECHNOLOGY

The first step in managing one's cyber risk is identifying what computers they need for education and development purposes. This process is going to be informed by what age group their child falls into. Some tablets may be appropriate for younger children, three to five years old, but a cell phone is inappropriate. The user also must understand that the more allowed devices translate into more devices that need to be managed. The same process should be considered for allowing children to have an email account and a profile on a gaming system or on a social network. Consider using Table 5.1 which is a general age guide for digital access. It is only a suggestion.

Children develop at very different rates. Parents should view this as a guide to what could be appropriate given the technology and their children's ages. It should not be considered a hard and fast rule.

Table 5.2 is a list of Web references for parents to gain additional understanding of technology and how to govern its use with their children. Once the user comes up with an approved device list, they can start planning how to manage the risk associated with each device.

TABLE 5.1 Parental Digital Device Age Guide

Age group	Device category	Appropriateness of device
3–8 years	Educational tablets	Tablets such as LeapFrog or Vtech, offer age-appropriate educational games and activities for young children.
6–12 years	Educational software	Computer software designed for children can provide fun and interactive learning experiences in various subjects, such as math, science, and language arts.
	Gaming consoles	Video game consoles such as the Nintendo Switch or PlayStation can provide entertainment and help children develop hand–eye coordination and problem-solving skills.
	Smartwatches	These devices offer basic features such as alarms, timers, and step counters while allowing for limited communication with parents.
8–16 years	Virtual reality headsets	These devices offer immersive experiences and can be used for educational purposes such as virtual field trips or interactive learning games.
	Digital cameras	Children can use digital cameras to explore their creativity and learn about photography.
	Child-friendly laptops	These laptops are designed for children, with pre-installed parental controls and educational software.
10–16 years	Smartphones	Smartphones can be helpful for older children to stay connected with family and friends and for educational purposes such as online resources.
	E-readers	These devices offer access to a wide range of digital books and can be a great way to encourage reading in older children.
	Podcasts	Listening to podcasts can be a fun and educational activity for children, with many podcasts geared toward kids on various topics such as science, history, and storytelling.

TABLE 5.2 Parent Web References

Parent reference	Web address
Common Sense Media: This Web site offers reviews and ratings of age-appropriate movies, TV shows, books, games, and apps for children.	*https://www.commonsensemedia.org/*
Family Online Safety Institute: This organization provides resources and tips for parents on how to keep their children safe online.	*https://www.fosi.org/*
Screenagers: This documentary film and Web site guides parents on navigating the digital world with their children.	*https://www.screenagersmovie.com/*
National PTA and Norton have put together *The Smart Talk*, a free tool that helps families set digital safety ground rules together.	*https://thesmarttalk.org/#/*
American Academy of Pediatrics: This organization provides guidelines on screen time and media use for children of different ages.	*https://www.healthychildren.org/English/ family-life/Media/Pages/Default.aspx*

FOUR BASIC PROCESSES FOR MANAGING CYBER RISK

There are four basic processes for managing a user's child's cyber risk: Control Devices, Restrictions, Monitoring, and Periodic Checking.

Controlling Devices

If the device is not needed, don't purchase it in the first place. That is straightforward, but families frequently have more than one child in a particular age group. The user must consider that one child may decide to allow a younger sibling to access the device they are not permitted to use. The user must consider how they are going to prevent that from occurring. Don't allow devices into the home unless one is prepared to address all the risks that they may represent to the user's entire family.

Restrictions

Restrictions include two kinds: verbal/written agreements and technological enforcement. Earlier discussed pledges may lay out use time frames or device prohibitions. Whether one decides to draw up written agreements or have verbal agreements on restrictions is up to the user and their family's needs for formality.

Technological restrictions include such things as setting up specific user accounts on family computers with parental controls, imposing parental controls on other devices, using passwords, restricting new software/hardware to be installed, and router configurations.

Adding Restrictions on Windows 11

Parents can go to Microsoft's Web site at *https://www.microsoft.com/en-us/microsoft-365/family-safety* to learn about how to add restrictions to Windows 11.

Parents can go on the computer to:

Settings > *Accounts* > *Family & Other Users* > *Family* **and click on** *Add Someone*

Consistent with Microsoft's requirements the user and their child will both need Microsoft accounts (not local accounts on the computer).

Monitoring

Monitoring can be as simple as requiring the child to use the device in a public area of the home where they can be actively supervised. It can also be technological in nature, specifically using monitoring software/hardware to record what they do for later review. Later in this chapter, issues regarding technological monitoring are discussed.

Periodic Checking

The final process involves periodically checking to ensure the user's child has not found a way to bypass the agreement and restrictions one has put in place. The simplest of these is ensuring the restricted device is where it should be. More intrusive steps may include checking browser search histories, which can be accessed through a browser's *History* tab. For the location of this tab conduct a Google search (Browser name + search history). Checking router logs is also an option but requires logging to be on and knowledge of the user's router's operation. Don't forget to ask questions about one's child's use, including on devices the user doesn't control, such as at a friend's home.

IDENTIFY PROGRAMS INSTALLED ON THE DEVICE

In today's world, phone apps are everything to many teenagers and children. Not so long ago, Vine, a video app, was popular; today, it's TikTok (which may be banned in the United States). Sharing personal stories and pictures on Instagram is popular, too. Many game apps are popular, as well as various instant messaging apps. Often, the user's physical location in the world defines the apps one can use. As a parent, reviewing the apps is necessary to protect one's children using technology that may lead to their harm from others. Has the user looked at their children's phone and opened all the apps to see what they are? Some devices have apps, such as

"Calculator#," that seem innocent, but upon opening the application, one quickly realizes that the app is not a calculator but a means to hide communications from parents. If one has parental control of the device, they should be able to limit the download of the app or the installation of new apps. Following is a listing of those apps that users need to be aware of that their children might be using without understanding the danger. This is not an exhaustive list, but it will hopefully give an idea of the kinds of risks/issues associated with these apps. Table 5.3 reflects the apps in no order of preference.

TABLE 5.3 Problematic Apps Parents Need to Know

App	What kind of app is it?	Why should a parent be concerned?
Tor and I2P	Provides access to the Dark Web.	Access to drugs and other adult material.
Tik Tok	Users share personal videos.	Access to pornography may be limited in the United States This is due to recent state level legislative changes.
WhatsApp	Communication (online phone, text, video chat)	Difficult to control content.
Kik	Provides group or private messages.	No age limit is applied by the vendor. Vendor messages are deleted after forty-eight hours, and it is difficult to monitor.
Snapchat	Group or private messages, videos, and photos.	Difficult to monitor.
Blendr, Tinder, MeetMe, and Hot or Not	Online adult dating apps that allow for messaging and exchange of photos and videos.	Children can upload personal information and pictures to adult sites leading to potential meeting of adults from the site. Hot or Not can also lead to a cyberbullying risk due to "rating" system.
Calculator#	Secret app	An app used to hide communications from parents looking at the children's phones.

The user must make some decisions if they find an app that might not be appropriate or that might endanger their children. First, don't panic. Research the app and find out what it does. Downloading the app and finding out about its social media aspects can be enlightening. Going on a dating app if one is in a relationship would be problematic without first checking with a partner. The user might want to consider following / friending their kids online to see into their world. Don't post on their pages. Talk with them if there is an issue found. Use this conversation to resolve your concerns.

Social Media

Due to the Children's Online Privacy Protection Act [COPPA\ of 1998 [COPPA 1998], the most popular social networks, such as Facebook, require a person to be at least thirteen years of age to open an account. COPPA is a US law that prohibits any organization or person operating online services (including social media services) to collect the personal information of anyone under the age of thirteen without parental permission. To avoid the parental permission requirements, these online services decided to just prohibit those under the age of 13 from having an account. The General Data Protection Regulation (GDPR) [European Union 2016] applies to online services covering Europe for minors less than sixteen years of age, although depending upon the member country, it can be as low as thirteen years of age. The COPPA and GDPR provisions are crafted to protect minors' privacy rights and are not meant to provide safeguards against other cyber risks. This is why, as a parent, the user should not just accept that your thirteen-year or older minor is free from all danger because they can legally sign up for an account. Minors who lie about their age to obtain an account also risk the deletion of all data, such as pictures, if the online services find out they improperly obtained an account.

Individual States Regulating Social Media

In 2023, states in the United States began passing legislation requiring minors get consent from a parent or guardian to sign up for a social media account. Two notable examples were Ohio and Utah. [Ohio Legislature 2023, Utah Legislature 2023]. Utah's Social Media Regulation Act (SMRA) requires minors to get consent from a parent or guardian to sign up for a social media account. It also requires social companies to verify users' ages, and it enables parents to monitor the content their kids are seeing and posting. The law also provides a curfew, preventing minors from accessing their accounts between the hours of 10:30 p.m. and 6:30 a.m., unless granted permission by their parents or guardian. Lawsuits have been filed in both states and it is yet to be determined if the laws will stand or if other states and the federal government will enact similar measures.

Online Services Especially for Minors

There are online services that allow minors under the age of thirteen to have an account, provided they obtain parental consent. Just as minors may lie about their age to obtain an account beyond the age requirements, predators can infiltrate these services by nefarious means to gain access to the user's child. A site reserved for minors does not negate the need to monitor its use. A user must decide the appropriate age for their child to have access and what accounts they wish to approve. Remember, any account, even mainstream services like Facebook, can expose children to material the user would rather not have them see at a particular age.

Some additional things to consider with one's child's use of social media are similar to the user's security and privacy. Get a list of one's children's social media accounts and use Table 5.4 to help manage its use. Remember, the more accounts they have, the more work is involved in effectively managing their use. Table 5.4 is provided as a checklist for parents to guide them through the process of securing your children's social media use. Watching over our children is a complicated and ongoing issue when it comes to technology. We hope this checklist can provide some concepts to alleviate the stress of our children and social media use.

TABLE 5.4 Children's Social Media Privacy Checklist

Check item	Facebook	Instagram	Twitter	Other
Security Items				
Are they allowed on the social media site at their age?				
What are their passwords?				
Have they set up two-factor authentication?				
Do they have security questions/answers selected?				
Don't allow automatic logins.				
Privacy Items				
Review the basic information that is public.				
Remove profile information that the user doesn't want public (names, schools, and sports teams)				
Set the account to the least number of reviews by other persons (friends only, not public).				
Limit who can connect with the minors.				
Turn off geotagging and location identification.				
Check the ad settings and limit the ads.				
Remove third-party apps and don't allow logins using apps.				

CHILDREN AND USER AGREEMENTS

Home technology user agreements are a set of rules and guidelines that parents and children agree to follow when using technology at home. These agreements are important because they help establish expectations, set boundaries, and promote responsible technology use. Often, children are exposed to technology at a young age and may not understand the potential risks and consequences. By establishing a user agreement, parents can educate their children on safe and appropriate technology use while also setting guidelines for monitoring usage and addressing any issues that may arise.

Creating a user agreement should be a collaborative effort between parents and children, allowing for open communication and understanding between both parties. These agreements can cover a range of topics such as time limits, appropriate content, online safety, and consequences for breaking the rules. It is important for parents to regularly revisit and update the agreement as their children grow and technology evolves. By involving children in the process, they will gain a better understanding and ownership of their technology use. Table 5.5 provides online resources for parents looking to create a home technology user agreement.

TABLE 5.5 Parents' Online Guides to User Agreements

Reference	Web address
Common Sense Media's Family Media Agreement	*https://www.commonsensemedia.org/family-media-agreement*
Federal Trade Commission's Parent's Guide to Protecting Kids' Privacy Online	*https://www.consumer.ftc.gov/articles/0031-protecting-your-childs-privacy-online*
National Online Safety's Parent Online Safety Hub	*https://nationalcollege.com/categories/online-safety*
KidsHealth's Internet Safety	*https://kidshealth.org/en/parents/net-safety.html*
ConnectSafely's Parents' Guide to Kids and Tech	*https://connectsafely.org/parentguides/*

USING MONITORING SOFTWARE

Parents retain legal rights to enforce control and discipline their children. Monitoring software, including GPS tracking software, provides the ability to invade the user's child's privacy, which was not possible in generations past. Some of this surveillance capability is built into some parental controls, particularly on cell phone applications, and may seem at first glance something the user wants to utilize. This may, however, make one question whether they want to be a parent or a prison guard over their children's online experiences. Besides this important question, there are important legal ramifications that the user must consider.

Legal Issues

US federal and/or state wiretap laws, collectively referred to as Title III laws, prohibit the interception of "real-time" communication by someone not a party to the communication. Federal law provides a minimum privacy protection level, with some states providing greater protection. Many hear the word wiretap and think it refers only to the intercepting of a telephone call. US courts have determined that computer monitoring can be considered a wiretap. Title III laws contain both criminal and civil penalties for violations.

Besides legal processes, such as a court order or warrant, monitoring can occur with consent. There are two kinds of consent. The first is one-party consent, which is contained in federal law and thirty-eight state statutes. The other type is called two-party consent. This means that both parties to the communication have to consent to the monitoring for it to qualify for this exception. There are twelve states (California, Connecticut, Florida, Illinois, Maryland, Massachusetts, Michigan, Montana, Nevada, New Hampshire, Pennsylvania, and Washington) that require two-party consent.

Many may think that all that is needed is to get the child's consent to have their digital lives monitored with these applications. That may be okay, but as noted, there are states that require both parties to the communication to consent to being monitored. Suppose the user is in one of those two-party states, and they are a single parent. The child starts texting with a noncustodial parent. Will that noncustodial parent be okay with monitoring their communication with the child? Will they make an issue of it and bring legal action? If one lives in a single consent state and their child takes the device, such as a cell phone, into a two-party state on, say, a school trip or a holiday to visit relatives, any communication that occurs while in that state requires both parties' consent to the monitoring.

Other Issues

Monitoring software has other issues besides legal concerns. Not all devices, such as gaming systems, can have monitoring software installed. Most antivirus software, as well as firewalls, will disable or otherwise cause issues for monitoring software functions. It is, after all, spying software. This requires the user to authorize an exception for the monitoring software through their antivirus software and firewall. If an exception is created it opens an opportunity for someone else to install other monitoring software for nefarious purposes against the user or their family. If someone gains unauthorized access to the monitoring software results, they could obtain an enormous amount of information about the user and their family. Obtaining some monitoring applications, particularly low-cost or freeware, will cause more problems, such as the introduction of other malware on the user's system.

Monitoring software can produce tons of data to be reviewed. This data is multiplied by how many devices it is installed on. Depending on the application, it can also send alerts to the user on key events. If one has the alerts improperly configured, they will quickly get inundated with false positives. For instance, if user decided to get an alert every time their child visited a Web site with the word *sex* appearing, the user would get email alerts for news articles about sex discrimination, sex education, or with a title such as *The Battle of the Sexes*. Monitoring software has to be configured and data reviews handled properly, or it will quickly overwhelm one's intended purpose of managing your child's cyber risk.

Deploying Monitoring Software

1. If the monitoring application permits it choose features that block certain activities or only generate alerts if an attempt was made to overcome restrictions. Blocking can help alleviate concerns over inadvertently monitoring communication requiring two-party consent by stopping the communication altogether.

2. Inform the child that monitoring software has been deployed on their devices. This may discourage them from bad behavior or may drive them to a nonmonitored device.

3. Avoid capturing everything if it is not needed. For instance, if one is worried about pornographic browsing, there is no need to capture Web-based email.

4. Set monitoring to trigger on key events such as pornographic Web sites. Some monitoring programs have predefined lists of problematic sites. This further limits the scope of one's monitoring.

5. Consider only capturing outgoing communication, as your child has presumably consented to the monitoring.

Final Thoughts on Monitoring Software

We are not here to recommend or disapprove monitoring applications. They are an invasion of privacy and should be carefully considered before including them in one's efforts to manage their child's cyber risk. They should not be a standard process for every household. The user is definitely better off if they can use restrictions as opposed to active monitoring. In some extreme situations, such as cases where the child has either been a cyberoffender or a cybervictim, particularly bullying, it may be justified. The user is encouraged to consider all the caveats that have been discussed and seek legal guidance before deploying this extreme management measure on their child's devices.

EDUCATING CHILDREN ON SOCIAL MEDIA PASSWORDS

The user's children are likely on social media, even if they say they are not. A brief search on Instagram or Pinterest will probably find their pages. Kids today mostly avoid Facebook. Some accounts there are just to satisfy their parents that they are not doing anything online to be concerned with. The best thing to do is start early with them about password usage on their accounts. Give them the lessons learned in Chapter 4 about passwords. Tell them not to share their passwords. As we know, childhood friends today can be enemies tomorrow. Password sharing can be emotionally detrimental when someone fakes the user's child's posts and says or does something mean or embarrassing. As we have seen in the past, it doesn't have to be the children. Parents can be just as mean and callous (or even criminal) toward other children online. Users need to stress to their children to immediately change their password if there is a data breach and not wait for a notice from the social media provider to do it. It should also be stressed not to keep their password written down on paper or a sticky note on their computer.

CRIMES CHILDREN ENCOUNTER ONLINE

Online victimization is not limited to adults. Children can fall for and are subject to a variety of scams and criminal offenses. Parents need to be ever vigilant not only on the playground but in the virtual environments our children play. The following are a few of the possible offenses to be aware of:

Cyberbullying. Bullying of any kind is detrimental to our children. Bullying on the Internet can be overwhelming and unusually harmful. Children today spend so much time on their technology that encountering someone who can be mean is probably more likely than not. Bullying that commences offline, such as in school, can be even more harmful when it includes online harassment. Bullying victims targeted offline and online can never get a break from the abuse, even in their own homes.

Cyberpredators. There are both men and women on the Internet that prey on our children. These predators may try and physically meet a child, but some, through trickery and blackmail, convince children to expose themselves for financial gain. Tragically, there have been sex extortion cases where the victim commits suicide. The National Center for Missing & Exploited Children (NCMEC) has an interactive experience, *No Escape Room (https://noescaperoom.org/)* that exposes parents and caregivers to the real-world threat from financial sextortion of minors [NCMEC 2024].

Phishing. This term refers to people(s) who use email messages to trick a receiver into clicking on a link or attachment that has malicious content which can lead to data and identity theft and fraud.

Other Online Considerations

Things posted on social media can remain on the Internet for years. Something the user's child posted a few years ago might not be socially acceptable today. Teaching children to protect themselves includes not posting material that is inflammatory, sexual, or bigoted. It can't be stressed enough that minors need to be careful what they post online.

Make sure children are aware that schools also often have policies about posting online content. Information posted online, even outside of school, can result in discipline if it violates school rules.

Children also need to understand that not everything that appears online is fact. This is a hard one even for adults. At a young age children need to learn to be cautious about what they see online. This is going to be harder as artificial intelligence is increasing being used to manipulate images and videos or fabricate stories. The implications of not being more critical of online posts should be apparent. Recently, a young female student was caught carrying a knife to school. When asked why she was carrying a knife she replied that there were posts on a social media site cautioning young women to be careful as it was *National Rape Day*. She was carrying the knife as she was expecting to be attacked due to this fictitious occasion.

The above incident is less likely to occur if the child understands they can come to a parent if they see something online that is questionable or just not right. This requires the parent to have a discussion defining problem material, which can range from bullying toward them or others, threatening violence, suicide ideations or threats, or sexually explicit posts.

MONITORING CHILDREN'S ONLINE ACTIVITIES

In today's digital age, it is crucial for parents to closely monitor their children's online activities. With the vast amount of information and content available on the Internet, there are also risks and dangers that children may be exposed to. It is important for parents to be aware of where their children go online and what they are doing in order to protect them from potential online scams and predators. By monitoring their children's online activities, parents can better guide and educate them on safe Internet practices, as well as identify any red flags or warning signs that may indicate their child is being targeted by scammers or other malicious individuals.

Monitoring where one's children go and what they are doing online is only one of the methods to ensure others don't take advantage of them online. The other is to educate them on the following:

1. Be selective when accepting friends, posting, and clicking. Don't accept requests from individuals they don't know, even those who appear to be children.

2. Think twice before they post. Remember posts can have a very long shelf life and can literally be seen by anyone.

3. Be careful where they check in from.

4. Don't share personal information online.

5. Don't send pictures to others, even if they know them. This one is harder than we think because kids post everything online.

6. Be mindful of phishing scams.

7. Don't use social media credentials to sign into third-party sites.

8. Avoid quizzes and games that require access to profile information.

9. Don't believe everything that is posted online. Verify information with multiple sources and check with a trusted adult about the information.

10. Make them cautious about groups or causes they follow. Joining or following inappropriate groups, such as those who are racist or extremist, can impact their lives later in life.

INSTILLING GOOD CELL PHONE HABITS

The best current parenting advice is to have a routine of making the child plug the phones, tablets, and computers into charge at night in a common area. No sleeping with the devices. This is tough; failure is inevitable without coparent discipline on this issue. There is no reason for kids to go to bed with a cell phone. Consider adding language to the home technology user agreement about cell phone usage, including no usage after bedtime, no usage at the dinner table at home, or in a restaurant, and where the device is to be maintained after bedtime. Table 5.6 is provided as a checklist for parents to guide them with your children's use of cellular telephones. Again, watching over our children is a complicated and ongoing issue. Cellular telephones today are small computers that provide children with connections around the world. This checklist is intended to provide some considerations for helping parents educate their children with the safety concepts required to prevent them from becoming a victim on their phones.

TABLE 5.6 Parent Checklist for Monitoring Children Online

	Item to address	Completed
1.	Set rules and boundaries for Internet usage, including time limits and guidelines for appropriate content.	
2.	Consider installing parental control software to restrict access to certain Web sites or content.	
3.	Regularly check the browser history to see which Web sites your child has been For cell phones also randomly check text messages and contacts to see who they are messaging and about what subjects.	
4.	Talk to your child about the potential dangers of sharing personal information online.	
5.	Teach your child to never click on suspicious links or pop-ups.	
6.	Monitor your child's social media accounts and set privacy settings to limit who can see their posts.	
7.	Teach your child to use strong and unique passwords for their online accounts.	
8.	Encourage your child to communicate to you or a trusted adult if they encounter something online that makes them uncomfortable.	
9.	Regularly review your child's contacts, friend lists and groups they join on social media platforms.	
10.	Keep communication lines open with your child and have frequent discussions about their online activities.	

RED FLAGS TO LOOK OUT FOR WITH CHILDREN

Make sure children know that they can talk to the parent and especially show any bad behavior they observe or is directed toward them. It is easier to intervene and help them through the situation than after something horrid has occurred. When they do not talk to us, we have to look for signs that they are being abused by someone online. Table 5.7 provides a noninclusive list of possible common red flags that children might exhibit if they have experienced online abuse.

TABLE 5.7 Warning Red Flags with Your Children

	Red flag	Constantly observing for
1.	Your child is spending *more time* than usual online, texting, gaming, or using social media apps.	
2.	Or, your child is spending a lot *less time* than usual online, texting, gaming or using social media apps.	
3.	Being secretive (more than normal) about: ■ to whom they are talking ■ what they're doing online ■ what they are doing on their smart phone ■ hiding their smart phone	

	Red flag	Constantly observing for
4.	Suddenly blocking you (or other family members) on social media.	
5.	Your child seems distraught (even angry or fearful) or distant from you other family and friends after being on social media, texting, or emailing.	
6.	The sudden appearance on their smart phone, laptop, or tablet of: • new phone numbers • new text messages • new email addresses • new communication apps	
7.	There is a sudden change in behavior toward school and favorite activities.	
8.	Your child isolates from family and friends.	
9.	You notice changes in your child's eating, sleeping, and/or spending patterns or habits.	
10.	There are instances of self-harm, such as cutting themselves and/or suicidal ideations.	

The parent knows their child best. If they do come to you with an issue from something that occurred online, listen, encourage them that they have done the correct thing and take them seriously. Depending on what has occurred, notifying the proper authorities can be warranted. The social media platform might be contacted to address any ongoing abuse. Keep in mind that all the social media platforms will have a different procedure and that procedure might include contacting the offender. Weigh carefully whether to contact the social media company before contacting law enforcement. It is never a good idea to contact the offending person. Leave that to law enforcement.

Additional Considerations

Juvenile sexting entails youths sending or posting sexually suggestive text messages and images, including nude or seminude photographs, via cellular telephones or over the Internet. [Bowker and Sullivan 2010] Pornographic images of minors, even if taken by the minor themselves, are illegal. Minors who send such images can leave a digital trail that comes back to a parent or guardian as they are the Internet account holder. Anyone who has possession of such contraband images can face legal consequences. For this reason, parents or legal guardians who detect such images should seek legal guidance.

CONCLUSION

Technology has changed how we view the security of our children. This chapter provided guidance on how to protect our children when they use technology. Whether it's computers, smartphones, or social media, we need to protect our children from the possible evils they may encounter. Chapter 6 will discuss how we can protect vulnerable adults who may not understand technology, or the risks associated with going online.

REFERENCES

Bowker, A., and Sullivan, M. "Sexting: Risky actions and overreactions." *FBI Law Enforcement Bulletin,* July 1, 2010. *https://leb.fbi.gov/articles/featured-articles/ sexting-risky-actions-and-overreactions*

Children's Online Privacy Protection Act of 1998, 15 U.S.C. 6501–6505. *https://www.ftc.gov/legal-library/browse/rules/childrens-online-privacy- protection-rule-coppa*

European Union. 2016. Regulation (EU) 2016/679 of the European Parliament and of the Council of 27 April 2016 on the protection of natural persons with regard to the processing of personal data and on the free movement of such data, and repealing Directive 95/46/EC (General Data Protection Regulation). *Official Journal of the European Union,* L 119/1. *https://eur-lex.europa.eu/eli/ reg/2016/679/oj*

The National Center for Missing & Exploited Children. 2024. "No escape room launches with new data." NCMEC Blog, April 16, 2024. *https://www.missing- kids.org/blog/2024/no-escape-room-launches-with-interactive-experience*

Ohio Legislature. 2023. *The Parental Notification by Social Media Operators Act. https://codes.ohio.gov/assets/laws/revised-code/authenticated/13/1349/1349.09/ 10-3-2023/1349.09-10-3-2023.pdf*

Utah Legislature. 2023. *Social Media Regulation Act (SMRA). https://le.utah. gov/~2023/bills/static/SB0152.html*

CHAPTER 6

PROTECTING ADULT FAMILY MEMBERS

IN THIS CHAPTER

This chapter discusses concepts of caring for the adult vulnerable family members who are not necessarily capable of dealing with cyberissues. Topics include methods for protecting them from cybercrime, dealing with the aftermath of a cyberattack, and handling social media after they pass on.

THE RISK TO VULNERABLE ADULTS IS REAL

In 2024, the Federal Bureau of Investigation (FBI) Internet Crime Complaint Center (IC3) reported 2023 losses by those over the age of sixty topped $3.4 billion, an almost 11% increase in reported losses from 2022. There was also a 14% increase in complaints filed with IC3 by elderly victims. [Federal Bureau of Investigation 2024]

Protecting vulnerable adult family members (senior citizens and disabled adults) in the digital world can't be overstated. As the world's population begins to age, the number of older adults online is increasing. We often hear more about the issues with younger people and online risks. Overlooked are the numbers of older people on social media and the harm they face. They are using their computer, their smartphone, and their tablets to access all kinds of resources that can expose them to cyber risks.

Vulnerable adult members are more trusting, particularly of government agencies, which makes them easy prey to schemes involving fraudsters pretending to be the government or convincing them to otherwise trust them. For a variety of reasons, they may feel isolated and lonely. These feelings of loneliness and isolation make them easy marks for criminals to manipulate them with attention and false praise. Their declining and/or limited mental/physical health due to age or illness affects their ability to suspect or detect another's evil intent. They are also unfamiliar with technology. These factors coupled with the possibility they have financial assets/

resources makes them a very inviting target for cybercriminals. Criminal elements recognize these factors and will not hesitate to exploit them for their own benefit. Family members need to develop a plan to aid them and protect them from these cyber risks.

COMMON ONLINE THREATS

Some of the more common threats to vulnerable adult family members are many of the same ones encountered by the rest of the population. Some threats seem specifically to target susceptible adults, such as identity theft. With the increasing use of technology and online transactions, it has become easier for scammers to steal personal and financial information. Vulnerable adults may not be as tech-savvy as younger generations, making them more susceptible to giving away their personal information to fake Web sites or parties they do not know.

Online threats come in various forms. These often lead to financial losses, can compromise personal information, and can negatively affect a vulnerable adults' mental/emotional well-being. It is essential to be educated about these threats and how they operate. Table 6.1 lists some of these threats. Table 6.2 provides Web sites that provide more details about these threats, emerging trends, and/or methods for reporting and addressing them.

TABLE 6.1 Types of Online Threats

Type	Definition
Identity theft	Identity theft is a crime during which someone uses another person's personal information, such as their name, social security number, credit card number, or other identifying information, without their permission to commit fraud or other crimes. This can lead to financial loss and damage to the victim's reputation and credit.
Online scams	Online scams use the Internet to deceive victims into giving away their money, personal information, or sensitive data. These scams can take various forms, including fake Web sites/profiles, phishing emails, telephone calls or social media or text messages. Social engineering tactics are often used to trick victims into giving away money or personal information. They often promise unrealistic rewards or benefits. They can also involve threats to convince the victim that if they don't take some action some financial or legal harm will befall them. These scams often involve impersonating a legitimate organization or authority and using fear or urgency to pressure victims into taking immediate action. Fake tech support, investment and cryptocurrency, Medicare and healthcare, romance, and grandparent scams described in this table are specific examples of these schemes.
Fake tech support scams	These fraudulent schemes involve scammers impersonating technical support from legitimate companies, such as Microsoft or Apple, and tricking victims into giving them access to their computer or personal information. This scam can also manifest in the form of pop-up warnings on Web sites, urging the victim to call a fake tech support number. If pop-up warnings are showing, run a scan of the system as it may be infected. Fake pop-ups are also an indication that the user was visiting a Web site that is either infected or is untrustworthy. If the system is up to date, pop-up scams should be greatly minimized. Scams can lead to financial loss or identity theft.

Type	Definition
Investment and cryptocurrency scams:	These fraudulent schemes promise huge and unrealistic returns on investment. They will often convince the target they are an expert, or they know a trusted individual who is advising them. They use fake Web sites, social media accounts, reports, screen shots, and emails to establish the investment is real and a great value. This is all false. They range from investments in high-risk stocks/bonds, to gold markets and digital currencies, such as Bitcoin. They trick victims into investing money. Once invested the fraudsters will provide bogus information to show the victim their investment is growing, to entice them into investing further. Victims will not recover their investment or any fictitious profits.
Medicare and healthcare scams:	Medicare and healthcare scams target elderly and vulnerable individuals by promising false or unapproved medical treatments or services. These scams can also involve identity theft, where scammers use stolen information to bill Medicare for fake services or equipment.
Romance scams:	Romance scams are a type of online scam where fraudsters create fake profiles on dating Web sites or social media platforms to establish romantic relationships with unsuspecting victims. These scams often involve grooming victims for weeks or months before asking for money, often for fictitious investment schemes or personal information under false pretenses. Failing to convince the victim to forward money or personal information, sexual banter may occur to convince vulnerable adults to forward nude images for extortion schemes.
Grandparent scams	This is one of the most common types of scams targeting older adults. In this scam, the elderly individual receives a call from someone pretending to be their grandchild or other relative in distress. The caller pretending to be the loved one claims to have been in a car accident, arrested, or in need of urgent financial assistance. In these cases, the scammers often use information found on social media or other public sources to make their story sound more convincing. They then request that the victim send money immediately through wire transfers, gift cards, or prepaid debit cards, making it difficult to track and recover the funds once they have been sent. Artificial intelligence (AI) may be used to impersonate loved ones to make the messages requesting financial assistance more believable. Consider adopting a password or password phrase for communicating with loved ones that can't be guessed for ensuring the user is actually speaking to the real person and not an AI created voice.
Cyberharassment	Cyberharassment is the act of harassing, intimidating, or threatening someone using electronic communication tools such as social media, text messages, or online forums. It can take many forms, including spreading rumors, sharing embarrassing or private information, or sending hurtful or threatening messages. Some users (trolls) will repeatedly post negative messages on other's posts. Cyberbullying is a subset of cyberharassment. Cyber-stalking is also another type, which can involve real-world stalking.
Sextortion	A crime often targeting minors can also have vulnerable adults as victims. The victim is tricked by another to send sexually explicit images Shortly after receiving the images the victim will be told they will send them to friends, the names of whom have been obtained from social media profiles, unless they send money, gift cards, and so on.
Malware and viruses	Malware and viruses are types of malicious software designed to exploit or damage a computer system or network. They can be unwittingly downloaded by users through infected emails, links, or downloads and can cause significant harm, such as stealing personal information, encrypting data, or causing system crashes.

TABLE 6.2 Resources on On-line Threats

Organization	Web site
American Association of Retired Persons (AARP)	https://www.aarp.org/home-family/personal-technology/ https://www.aarp.org/money/scams-fraud/fraud-watch-network/ https://www.aarp.org/money/scams-fraud/
Better Business Bureau Scam Tracker	https://www.bbb.org/scamtracker/us
Cybercrime Support Network	https://cybercrimesupport.org/
FBI	https://www.fbi.gov/how-we-can-help-you/scams-and-safety/on-the-internet
FBI Internet Crime Complaint Center	https://www.ic3.gov/default.aspx
Federal Trade Commission (FTC)	https://www.ftc.gov/ https://consumer.ftc.gov/identity-theft-and-online-security
Identity Theft Resource Center	https://www.idtheftcenter.org/
IRS Identity Theft Central	https://www.irs.gov/identity-theft-central
The Consumer Financial Protection Bureau (CFPB)	https://www.consumerfinance.gov/
Medicare Fraud	https://www.medicare.gov/basics/reporting-medicare-fraud-and-abuse
National Adult Protective Services Association	https://www.napsa-now.org/financial-exploitation/
National Center for Missing and Exploited Children (NCMEC) Online Safety Tips for Adults	https://www.missingkids.org/netsmartz/resources
National Center on Elder Abuse	https://ncea.acl.gov/
National Council on Aging's Eldercare Locator	https://eldercare.acl.gov/Public/Index.aspx
National Foundation for Consumer Credit	https://www.consumercredit.com/
Scam Alert	http://www.scamalert.sg/
Social Security Administration	https://www.ssa.gov/fraud/
StaySafeOnline.org	https://staysafeonline.org/resources/online-safety-privacy-basics/

PREVENTION

All the steps previously suggested to strengthen systems are applicable to vulnerable adults' systems (computer, tablets, Kindle books, cell phones, etc.). Make sure their systems have up-to-date software and antivirus and antispyware installed. Also make sure their social media profiles settings are restricted too. Many of these threats can be stopped before they even appear to vulnerable adults by strengthening their defenses. Educate them about accessing the spam folder. They should only be exploring the spam folder for a specific email that they were expecting that got misidentified as a problem.

Be aware that many assisted living facilities will provide free Wi-Fi to their residents. Assess how secure the vulnerable adults' systems are in operating in that environment and take measures suggested in this book to tighten up the vulnerable adults' defenses. The next important step is to engage vulnerable adults on a regular basis about not only the cyber risks but about life in general. Isolation and feelings of loneliness are risk factors cybercriminals depend upon to exploit vulnerable adults.

MONITORING FOR VULNERABLE ADULT SCAMS

These scams not only lead to financial losses for the victims but can also have a significant impact on their emotional well-being and independence. It is crucial for adult children or caregivers to be vigilant in monitoring scams targeting older adults and to take steps to prevent their loved ones from becoming victims. These scams often prey on the vulnerability and trust of older individuals, resulting in financial loss and emotional distress. To recognize and avoid scams, it is important to be aware of some common red flags that cybercriminals are targeting vulnerable adults. Vulnerable adults need to know that if something seems too good to be true or makes them feel uneasy, they need to stop and check with a trusted person who they personally know offline. They should feel comfortable asking for advice and do some research before giving out any information or making any payments. Stress the importance of only providing personal or financial information on secure and trusted Web sites, and never give out sensitive information over the phone unless they initiated the call. Table 6.3 is a checklist of red flags to discuss with vulnerable adults. Be aware prevention may also require setting up time to assist vulnerable adults communicating online when it deals with financial or medical concerns.

TABLE 6.3 Red Flag Discussions

	Red flag	Covered
1.	Emails or messages from unknown senders or companies they have not interacted with before. Included are unknown or untrustworthy callers.	
2.	Telephone calls or emails purportedly from government agencies, financial institutions, or utilities threatening some actions (liens, accounts being frozen/closed, or arrest) unless they take immediate actions. Government agencies do not communicate in this matter.	
3.	Unsolicited messages or emails asking for personal information, such as passwords, bank account numbers, or social security numbers.	
4.	Unsolicited requests for remote access to their computer.	
5.	Poor grammar and spelling in messages or emails.	
6.	Suspicious links or attachments in messages or emails.	
7.	Fake Web sites or social media profiles. Stress that fake social media profiles of friends and relatives can be created by cybercriminals.	
8.	Messages or emails claiming they won a prize or lottery that were not entered.	
9.	Unsolicited offers for investments or financial opportunities. Any offers that sound too good to be true.	
10.	Requests for advance fees, wire transfers, or use of prepaid debit or gift cards as payment.	
11.	Requests for immediate payment or pressure to act quickly including claims of a limited time offer or limited availability to pressure them into acting.	
12.	Threats or urgent messages claiming their account will be closed or suspended or messages with intimidating language, such as threats of legal action or account suspension.	
13.	Requests for personal information such as social security number, credit card numbers, or bank account information from unknown sources.	
14.	Unexpected charges on their credit card or bank account.	

Aside from monitoring for scams, it is also important to set boundaries for vulnerable adults' online activities. This can include limiting their access to financial accounts or setting up alerts for suspicious activity on their accounts. It is also important to stay involved in their financial affairs and to regularly check in with them about any potential scams they may have encountered. Staying involved can help prevent them from making any impulsive or uninformed decisions that could put them at risk. Regular checking bank and credit cards statements can detect irregularities and recover or minimize losses that may have occurred.

Openly talking about the various types of scams and warning signs empowers vulnerable adults to recognize and avoid potential scams on their own. It is also important to stay involved in their daily lives and to have regular conversations about their financial decisions and any change in their financial situation. This allows intervention should any red flags or concerning behavior be detected. Monitoring and setting boundaries do not mean isolating vulnerable family members from the Internet. Encourage them to ask for help or clarification from a trusted person they know if they receive any suspicious calls or emails. Staying involved in a vulnerable family member's financial decision is also crucial in preventing them from being exploited. If the user is unable to monitor their finances, consider appointing a trusted family member or financial advisor to help oversee their accounts.

Depending on the concern present the user may wish to consider installing monitoring software on their systems but only after careful consideration of legal concerns discussed in this book. Remember to report any suspected scams or cybercrimes to the appropriate authorities (see Tables 6.7 and 6.8). Seek help from trusted family members or professionals if the vulnerable family member has fallen victim to a scam. With vigilance and awareness, elderly loved ones can be made safe from these malicious schemes.

Noticing Behaviors Associated with Victimization

There are numerous behavioral red flags that may indicate a vulnerable family member is being targeted by a scammer. One major red flag is a sudden change in financial habits or patterns. For example, if a loved one was always careful with their money but suddenly begins making large, unusual purchases or giving away money to unfamiliar people, this could be a sign that they are being manipulated by a scammer. Another red flag is increased isolation or withdrawal from family and friends. Scammers often try to isolate their victims to gain their trust and control over their actions. If a loved one is becoming more secretive or distant, it is important to investigate further and make sure they are not being targeted by a scammer.

Another common behavioral red flag is a sudden change in personality or mental state. Scammers often use fear tactics or emotional manipulation to exploit their victims, which can lead to changes in behavior or mood. If a loved one becomes more anxious, fearful, or paranoid, it could be a sign that they are being attacked by a cybercriminal. If they seem confused or disoriented when discussing their finances or any recent interactions, this could also be a red flag. It is important to pay attention to any changes in a loved one's behavior and address them as soon as possible to protect them from potential scams or minimize the harm. Early detection of behavior changes due to victimization will help minimize the damage inflicted. Here are some specific changes that may indicate a family member has fallen victim to a scam:

- sudden financial difficulties
- increased secrecy about online activities
- spending time with a "new friend" they've met online
- querying about installing new communication apps on their smartphone
- expresses desire to travel out of the state or country to meet someone
- new interest in cryptocurrency
- believe that their wealth will soon increase

Difficult Conversations

No one wants to acknowledge they may have been fooled or tricked into making a mistake. It is a challenging and emotional task to discuss such matters with family members who may have been independent for most of their lives and may not be used to being vulnerable or dependent on others. They may feel embarrassed or ashamed about falling for a scam, making it difficult to be open and talk about the issue. Some may have cognitive impairments, making it harder for them to fully understand the situation and the potential consequences of their actions. They may also have a fear of losing their independence or pride, making them hesitant to admit when they have been taken advantage of. This can make it challenging to broach the subject of potential scams. These conversations can also be difficult because family members may feel guilty or responsible for not being able to protect their loved ones from being scammed. It can also be emotionally taxing to see a family member being taken advantage of, and it can be challenging to confront them about it.

Many of them may have grown up in a time where trusting others was the norm, and they may have a hard time accepting that there are people out there who are looking to take advantage of them. The embarrassment and shame that they feel for falling for what seems an obvious scam may prevent them from admitting the deception to their loved ones. They may feel defensive or refuse to discuss it altogether. Pride can make them stubborn to admit something is amiss. They may have a hard time accepting that they are no longer able to make decisions on their own or may not want to admit that they are being taken advantage of. These factors may make it hard to have a productive conversation. It is important for family members to approach these conversations with sensitivity and empathy, and to have patience and understanding for their vulnerable loved ones.

At-risk adults who live with the user might make it easier to recognize underlying issues with family members' cognitive/emotional concerns. Vulnerable adults living alone may make it harder to notice cognitive decline. Web sites such American Association of Retired Persons (AARP; *https://www.aarp.org/health/brain-health/alzheimers-and-dementiaas*) and the National Council on Aging's Eldercare Locator (*https://eldercare.acl.gov/Public/Index.aspx*) provide online resources to help in recognizing and dealing with cognitive decline.

There are times when it becomes necessary for users to recognize that they must assume full control over elder parents' finances due to their diminishing physical/mental abilities. Sometimes this can be accomplished with the voluntary cooperation of the elderly before they lose the ability to legally consent to such measures. It sometimes requires legal intervention through a probate court and formal guardianship. Users should consult with legal counsel for the best option that insures they can protect their family members.

Real Life Cybercrime Victims

It may be helpful to give vulnerable adults real examples of individuals like themselves who fell victim to cybercrimes. One of the biggest cybercrimes that are targeting the elderly is called *pig butchering*. When asked to provide a definition of pig butchering for this book, cybercrime and crypto expert Erin West stated the following:

> Pig butchering is the most devastating scam threat to financial and mental health to date. Emanating from organized crime in Southeast Asia, this crime combines the traditional elements of a romance scam and then super drives it by coercing victims to invest their entire net worth into a fake cryptocurrency platform. The term *pig butchering* comes from the Chinese *sha zu pan* and is meant to fatten up the victim with love bombing until they are eventually slaughtered, and all of their money is lost.
>
> It works like this: a scammer connects with a victim on a social media platform, moves to an encrypted conversation, and begins a months-long courtship where the scammer shows an enviable lifestyle of fancy travel and a high-end home and vehicle. They will text up to 4–5 hours a day. Our victim is led to believe they have found true love. The scammer then discloses that they have made their money through cryptocurrency and gets the victim to invest a small amount into a phony Web platform controlled by the scammer. The victim is shown exponential gains, and the scammer induces the victim to invest more and more, liquidating retirement and children's college accounts. Ultimately when the victim tries to remove the funds, the victim is hit with a 25% tax which requires new money. The victim will then take out high interest loans and a second mortgage, only to find out the entire affair was a scam. Victims in droves find themselves completely emotionally crushed and suffer the loss of their complete financial stability.

Erin West has been a 25-year Deputy District Attorney with the Santa Clara County Prosecutor's Office in California. She is assigned to the Regional Enforcement Allied Computer Team (REACT), which is a partnership of 17 local, state, and federal agencies, with the Santa Clara County District Attorney's Office designated as the lead agency. It is one of five such teams in California specifically created in 1997 to combat high tech crimes. *http://reacttf.org/10701.htm*

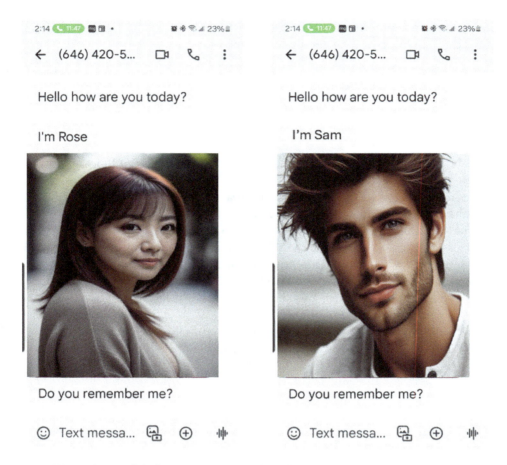

FIGURE 6.1 Unsolicited text message to start the pig butchering scam (images AI generated).

Figure 6.1 is a real message received via text messaging. This is a typical message intended to start a conversation, as Erin West described in the preceding extract, to prompt the receiver to engage in further conversations. A photo of a woman is often used to make the unsolicited message seem real and to try and put the receiver of the massage at ease.

The following real cases were pulled from U.S. Department of Justice press releases and demonstrate the fact that these schemes often involve multiple conspirators.

Four Individuals Charged for Laundering Millions from Cryptocurrency Investment Scams" [U.S. Department of Justice 2023]

A seven-count indictment was unsealed in Los Angeles charging four individuals for their alleged roles in a scheme to launder the proceeds of cryptocurrency investment scams and other fraudulent schemes involving millions of dollars in victim funds.

Court documents alleged the defendant conspired to open shell companies and bank accounts to launder victim proceeds of cryptocurrency investment scams, also known as *pig butchering*, and other fraudulent schemes. They transferred the funds to domestic and international financial institutions. The overall fraud scheme in the related pig-butchering syndicate involved at least 284 transactions and resulted in more than $80 million in victim losses. More than $20 million in victim funds were directly deposited into bank accounts associated with the defendants.

Four Accused of Nationwide Tech Support Fraud Scam Targeting the Elderly [U.S. Attorney's Office, Eastern District of Missouri, 2024]

An investigation commenced in August of 2023, after a seventy-eight-year-old Missouri man responded to a pop-up message claiming his computer was infected with a virus. The victim and his seventy-six-year-old wife were falsely told that their banking information had been compromised because someone had been accessing child pornography through the computer. To escape criminal prosecution, they were told they had to pay $88,000.

Following instructions in a series of text messages, the Missouri couple gathered the money, took photos of it and sealed it in a cardboard box. They were told to wait for a courier but began to be suspicious and balked when the courier arrived. They called the police, and the courier was arrested.

Charging documents say that courier was paid $500 to $1,000 to pick up cash from victims and use a counterfeit passport and fraudulently obtained debit card to deposit it into a bank. He then withdrew money in cashier's checks to send to coconspirators.

Investigators learned the leaders of the conspiracy provided couriers with assignments and instructions. Couriers were recruited from colleges. They fraudulently opened financial accounts using the names and passports of citizens of Taiwan.

About $7 million in cashier's checks were deposited into one bank account from this scheme between March 2020 and July 2023.

India-Based Computer-Hacking Scam that Targeted Elderly Across the Country [U.S. Attorney's Office, District of Montana, 2024]

A Montana federal judge sentenced an Indian national to four years and three months in prison for his role in stealing $150,000 from a Kalispell woman through an international computer-hacking scheme that targeted elderly Americans nationwide and resulted in more than $1.2 million in total losses. The man sentenced was a *phantom hacker*, individuals who "… layer imposter tech support, financial, and government personas to gain access to someone's computer and personal information" (para. 5). The scammer traveled overseas to collect the victim's money in person. Victim statements to the court revealed how this crime negatively affected the victims beyond the financial loss.

One victim statement stated "I feel very violated…I have crawled into a shell emotionally and don't want to be vulnerable in any way. I don't know who I can safely trust now. I don't feel safe at all" (para. 7). Another victim wrote "I'm driving a 2007 car, and this loss has prevented me from affording a new car. The cost of living keeps going up, which doesn't help when on a fixed income. I'm not sure I will ever have peace of mind again and trust others. This has cost me more than any monetary loss" (para. 8).

The government alleged in court documents that a large enterprise originating from India was involved in stealing $1,236,470 from elderly Americans. The Montana case arose in February 2023, when a bank notified the FBI of the fraud, in which a fraudster tricked a seventy-three-year-old victim into giving them money through a pop-up notice that appeared on her computer screen. The notice explained that Jane Doe had been *hacked* and for her to call a number for customer support. The victim complied, and fraudsters directed her to remove cash from her bank accounts for safe keeping at the *Fed*. She complied and gave $150,000 in cash to the fraudsters. The FBI set up a ruse and captured the fraudsters. The investigation determined that the fraudsters remotely accessed the victim's computer, using UltraViewer, which they had installed on her computer.

NAVIGATING SOCIAL MEDIA SAFELY FOR SENIORS

Navigating social media can be a fun and exciting way for seniors to stay connected with family and friends, but it's important to do so safely. The first step in protecting their social media usage is to manage their privacy settings. Make sure they only share personal information with friends and family and adjust their settings so that only approved connections can view their profile. Many platforms offer two-factor authentication, which requires a code or confirmation from a second device before logging in. This adds an extra layer of security to prevent hacking or unauthorized access to their accounts. The user may have to assist them with these settings and periodically check them to make sure they are properly set.

It's also important for them to be wary of friend requests from strangers and not to accept them without verifying the person's identity. It is equally important for them to be aware that fraudsters will create fake profiles of real friends/relatives.

Remind vulnerable adults that not everything they see on social media is true. With the rise of fake news and online hate speech, seniors may fall prey to false information and negative comments, leading to feelings of isolation and vulnerability. Social media has become a ubiquitous part of our daily lives, with people of all ages using various platforms to connect, share, and stay informed. While it can offer many benefits, such as staying connected with friends and family, it also comes with risks, especially for older adults. Seniors may not be as familiar with the technology and potential dangers associated with social media. It's essential for them to understand how to navigate these platforms safely. They need the time to fact check information before sharing or believing it. They need to be reminded to avoid posting sensitive or controversial topics and be respectful in their interactions with others. By following these safety tips, seniors can enjoy all the benefits of social media without compromising their personal information or safety. The following list of Social Media Safety Discussion Points provides key social media safety discussions points to cover with vulnerable adults. Table 6.4 discusses the kinds of topics to discuss with vulnerable adults when reviewing the topic of safety on-line.

TABLE 6.4 Social Media Safety Discussion Points

1	Create strong and unique passwords. Seniors should avoid using the same password for multiple accounts and should create a strong and unique password for each social media account. A password manager is especially important for aging seniors who may forget numerous passwords.
2	Be cautious about clicking on links or opening attachments from unknown sources. These could contain viruses or malware that can damage their devices or steal their information. These links can also lead to malicious Web sites where their system gets infected with malware. It's always safer to verify the source of the message before clicking on any links or downloading attachments.
3	Think before posting. Before sharing anything on social media, seniors should think about how it could potentially be used against them. This includes personal information, photos, and even location check-ins.
4	Be selective with friend requests. Seniors should only accept friend requests from people they know and trust. It is essential to be cautious of strangers who may try to establish a connection on social media. They also need to understand that fraudsters will create fake profiles in the names of friends/relatives to trick them into connecting.
5	Limit personal information. Seniors should be cautioned against sharing personal information such as their full name, address, phone number, or date of birth on social media platforms.
6	Be aware of fake news and scams. Older adults should be vigilant about fake news and scams circulating on social media. It is advisable to fact-check information before sharing or believing it.
7	Use reputable social media platforms. Seniors should stick to using reputable and well-known social media platforms to minimize the risk of scams and other issues. Dating-sites are frequently used by criminals to victimize victims with all manner of schemes. Scammers will try to convince their targets to continue their communications on message applications, such as WhatsApp or Telegram. These applications are used for fraudster's convenience and to further hide their tracks.

IDENTIFYING SCAMS

Despite taking precautions, vulnerable adults may still come across fake profiles, scams, or other concerning content while using social media. If they come across any suspicious activity or receive messages from unknown sources on social media, it is important to know how to identify and report them. For example, if someone receives a suspicious message from a friend or family member asking for money, they should verify the request's authenticity before sending any funds. They can do so by contacting the person directly through another means of communication, such as calling them or asking a trusted family member to verify they are seeking assistance. AI use by scammers will make this challenging. Social media platforms have dedicated reporting functions for fake profiles, scams, and other concerning content. Vulnerable adults should be aware of these functions and use them when necessary. Some red flags to watch out for on social media include:

- recently created profiles
- profiles with suspicious or no information and a limited number of friends
- unsolicited messages asking for personal information or money
- posts or messages with bad grammar or spelling mistakes
- requests for money, wire transfers, the purchase/transfer of digital currency or gift cards
- requests to exchange nude photos or videos, which can later be used for extortion of the vulnerable adult.

DEALING WITH POTENTIAL CYBERATTACKS/SCAMS

Discovering that an adult family member has fallen victim to a cyberattack or scam can be a stressful and concerning situation. It is important to stay calm and approach the situation with a level head. The first step in dealing with a potential incident is to gather all the information and details about what happened. This can include any suspicious emails, text messages, or phone calls that were received, as well as any financial transactions or personal information that may have been compromised. It is important to document everything and keep track of any evidence that may be needed for further investigation. If the victimization occurred on a social media platform document where it occurred and which profile(s) were involved. Capture all text/chat messages. Some programs allow users to download these. If not, users should take screenshots of the messages.

Once all the necessary information is collected, it is important to take immediate action to protect the victim and prevent any further damage. This may include contacting the financial institutions involved to freeze accounts or cancel credit cards, changing passwords and security questions on all online accounts, and notifying the appropriate authorities. (See Table 6.7 for US residences and Table 6.8 for outside the United States) It is also important to educate the victim on how to recognize and avoid future potential scams, as well as regularly monitoring their accounts for any suspicious activity. Last, offering emotional support and reassurance during this difficult time is crucial in helping the victim feel safe and secure. Table 6.5 is a Four step guide to helping recover from Identify Theft and Fraud. If you or your loved one become a victim consider these steps.

TABLE 6.5 Four Steps to Recovering from Identify Theft/Fraud

	Step	Action
1.	Contact financial institutions	As soon as identity theft or fraud is suspected, contact banks, credit card companies, and other financial institutions. Inform them about the suspicious activity and ask them to freeze accounts to prevent further unauthorized transactions.
2.	File a report with the authorities	File a report with the local police department or appropriate agency. (See Table 6.7 for US residents and Table 6.8 for outside the United States). This will help create an official record of the incident and may be necessary for future steps, such as disputing fraudulent charges or for insurance purposes.
3.	Review credit report	Request a copy of a credit report from one of the major credit bureaus. Chapter 9 contains the contacts for Equifax, Experian, or TransUnion as well as for those credit bureaus outside the United States. Review the report carefully for any unauthorized accounts or inquiries. If any discrepancies are detected dispute them with the credit bureau.
4.	Monitor your accounts and credit	It is important to monitor bank and credit card statements regularly for any unfamiliar charges or transactions. Consider placing a fraud alert or credit freeze on credit reports to prevent new accounts from being opened in your name without your knowledge. Consider signing up for a credit monitoring service to receive alerts on any suspicious activity on the credit report.

REPORTING TO THE PROPER AUTHORITIES

Reporting cyberschemes can help prevent others from falling victim to the same scam and can also aid in the investigation and prosecution of scammers. It is important to take swift action when someone has been targeted by a scam and to report it to the proper authorities. Table 6.6 provides the steps to reporting an on-line crime to law enforcement. Review these steps if you or your loved one become a victim.

TABLE 6.6 Reporting Scams to the Authorities

Step	Description
Gather all necessary information	Before reporting a scam, it is important to have all the relevant details about the scammer and the scam itself. This includes any communication or documentation received, as well as the name, contact information, and any other identifying information of the scammer.
Contact the appropriate authorities	If the scam involves financial fraud, contact the local police department. In the United States also report it to the Federal Trade Commission (FTC) or the Consumer Financial Protection Bureau (CFPB). If it is an online scam, report it to the Internet Crime Complaint Center (IC3). For scams related to identity theft, contact the Federal Trade Commission (FTC) or the Social Security Administration (SSA). For cases involving federal tax refunds schemes contact the Internal Revenue Service (IRS).
File a report	Most of these authorities have online complaint forms that can be filled out to report the scam. These forms usually ask for the details of the scam, the scammer's information, and contact information. Make sure to provide as much detail as possible in the report.
Follow up	After filing a report, it is important to follow up with the authorities to ensure that the report has been received and that they are taking appropriate action. Ask for a case or reference number for the report, which will help track the progress of the investigation.
Report to the relevant financial institution	If the scam involved a fraudulent transaction on a credit or debit card, report it to the bank or credit card company immediately. They may be able to reverse the transaction and prevent further fraudulent charges.
Inform others	Scammers often target multiple victims, so it is important to warn others about the scam. Report the scam to consumer protection agencies, sharing the experience on social media, or write reviews on Web sites that track scams and frauds.
Be cautious of follow-up scams	After reporting a scam, the victim may receive follow-up calls or emails from scammers pretending to be from the authorities. They may ask for more personal information or money to help resolve the scam. Be cautious of these follow-up scams and always verify the legitimacy of the contacting person.
Place fraud alerts through all the credit reporting agencies and ask for credit reports.	See Chapter 9 for a discussion on credit monitoring versus freezing and the associated tables for listing of credit bureaus.

TABLE 6.7 Reporting Cybercrimes in the United States

Local/State	
Google Search: Local Police or Sheriff's Department – [city/town name] + Police Department (ex: Cleveland, Ohio Police Department)	
Google Search: State Attorney General's Office – [state name] + Attorney General's Office (e.g., Nevada Attorney General's Office)	
Federal	
Consumer Financial Protection Bureau (CFPB)	*https://www.consumerfinance.gov/complaint/*
Federal Bureau of Investigation (FBI) Internet Crime Complaint Center (IC3)	*https://www.ic3.gov/*
Federal Trade Commission (FTC)	*https://reportfraud.ftc.gov/#/*
Internal Revenue Service	*https://www.irs.gov/identity-theft-central*
Medicare Fraud	*https://www.medicare.gov/basics/reporting-medicare-fraud-and-abuse*
Social Security Administration	*https://www.ssa.gov/fraud/*
U.S. Postal Inspection Service (USPIS)	*https://www.uspis.gov/report*

TABLE 6.8 Reporting Cybercrimes Outside the United States

Reporting mechanisms vary from one country to another. Some countries have a dedicated online option in place and others advise the party to go to their local police station to lodge a complaint. Individuals may have to start with their local police department if their country is not listed in this table.	
Australia	
Cybercrime:	*https://www.cyber.gov.au/report-and-recover/report*
Identify Theft:	*https://www.scamwatch.gov.au/report-a-scam*
Canada	
Cybercrime	*https://www.cyber.gc.ca/en/incident-management*
Identity Theft	*https://www.priv.gc.ca/en/privacy-topics/identities/identity-theft/guide_idt/*
European Union	
Cybercrime	*https://www.europol.europa.eu/report-a-crime/report-cybercrime-online*
Fraud	*https://anti-fraud.ec.europa.eu/olaf-and-you/report-fraud_en*
Israel	
Cybercrime	*https://www.gov.il/en/departments/general/contact#:~:text=Computer%20 Emergency%20Response%20Center%20(CERT,119%20%7C%20Israel%20 National%20Cyber%20Directorate*
Identity Theft	*https://www.btl.gov.il/English%20Homepage/stations/Call%20Centers/Pages/ reporting-fraud.aspx*

Japan	
Cybercrime/Fraud	*https://japanantifraud.org/report-a-fraud-in-japan/#:~:text=If%20you%20 have%20been%20scammed,Center%20of%20Japanese%20Police%20 Department.&text=Please%20leave%20this%20field%20empty,human%20by%20 selecting%20the%20cup.*
New Zealand	
Cybercrime	*https://www.police.govt.nz/advice-services/cybercrime-and-internet*
Identity Theft	*https://www.scamwatch.gov.au/report-a-scam*
United Kingdom	
Fraud and Cybercrime	*https://www.actionfraud.police.uk/*
Identity Theft	*https://ico.org.uk/for-the-public/identity-theft/*

HELPING VULNERABLE ADULTS RECOVER FROM ONLINE SCAMS

It is crucial to provide emotional support and reassurance to the victim. Being scammed can leave older adults feeling embarrassed, guilty, and vulnerable. Show them empathy and understanding and let them know that it is not their fault. Encourage them to talk about their experience and listen attentively without judgment. This will help them process their emotions and move on from the incident. Recovering from an online scam can be a difficult and overwhelming experience for older adults. They may feel humiliated, violated, and even experience financial loss. As a loved one or caregiver, it is important to provide emotional support and reassurance to help them cope with the situation. Encourage them to talk about their feelings and let them know that they are not at fault for falling for the scam. It is important to listen without being critical and be understanding of their emotions.

Additionally, help them report the scam to the appropriate authorities. This will not only give them a sense of control but also help prevent the scammer from targeting others. Last, support them in taking necessary precautions to protect themselves from future scams, such as changing their passwords and being cautious of suspicious emails or calls. Taking these steps plays a vital role in helping older adults recover from an online scam and prevent them from falling victim again.

DIGITAL LEGACY AND AFTERLIFE PLANNING

The importance of digital legacy planning for adult family members, including seniors, who may not be familiar with technology is an important concept to understand. Make sure your loved ones have a proper estate plan in place. This includes a will, power of attorney, and advanced healthcare directives. Emphasize the need to designate a digital executor and provide them with necessary login information for accounts and devices. Discuss the importance of creating a digital will, which includes information on how to access and close all online accounts. Highlight the potential risks of leaving personal information and accounts open after passing away, such as identity theft and fraudulent activity. Provide tips on how to securely transfer ownership of digital assets and accounts after a family member's passing, including using password managers and updating online wills.

Creating a digital estate plan is essential in ensuring that digital assets are properly managed and distributed after one's passing. This includes all of one's online accounts, such as social media, email, and financial accounts, as well as any digital files or documents with sentimental or monetary value. With a digital estate plan, these assets may be recovered. Without such a plan they may become inaccessible or fall into the wrong hands. It is essential to carefully consider who one wants access to their digital assets and how they want them to be handled after one can no longer manage themselves.

Start by making an inventory of all digital assets, including online accounts, social media profiles, and other important digital information. It would help if one designated a digital executor, someone trusted to handle one's digital assets according to their wishes. The digital executor or trustee will manage digital assets according to the user's wishes. This may include providing them with access to passwords, login information, and instructions on handling the accounts after one's death. One can also specify whether they want their digital assets to be passed down to loved ones, donated to a charity, or deleted after passing. It is also essential to regularly review and update the digital estate plan, as one's digital presence, assets and passwords may change over time.

It is essential to think about the practical aspects of accessing the accounts and the emotional impact on loved ones. In addition to important information, digital versions often hold memories and sentimental value, such as photos and messages. Therefore, it is essential to discuss with loved ones which accounts, and information should be passed on and how they want it handled.

It is important to understand that computers contain vast amounts of very personal information. In some ways they can be *windows to a person's soul*. They may contain information of past indiscretions or infidelity, or questionable interests, even illegal material. The illegal material referred to is child pornography. This material is illegal to look for or even to possess. The user needs to seek legal advice if this kind of material is discovered, which may lead to contacting law enforcement. Failure to hand off this material to the proper authorities can have legal implications for the one who possesses it.

Another consideration is the security and privacy of digital accounts. It is essential to carefully consider with whom one shares account information and the level of access they will have. Consider the potential risks of sharing this sensitive information and take necessary precautions, such as using strong and unique passwords and enabling two-factor authentication. Be aware of any legal or financial implications arising from sharing account information and seek legal advice if needed. Ultimately, careful consideration and planning are crucial to ensuring digital accounts and passwords are passed on securely and responsibly.

Closing a Deceased Family Member's Social Media Accounts

Losing a loved one is never easy, and in today's digital age, the process of mourning and closure has taken on new dimensions with the prevalence of social media. Many use social media platforms to document and share their lives, creating a digital presence that can continue long after they are gone. When a family member passes away, their accounts can become a source of pain and risk if not correctly handled. Leaving social media accounts open after a family member's death can pose various risks and dangers. One of the most significant concerns is identity theft. Hackers and scammers can use the deceased's personal information and photos on their social media accounts to create fake profiles or access sensitive information. Leaving the accounts open can cause financial damage and tarnish the deceased's online reputation. Moreover, leaving these accounts open can also lead to privacy breaches, where strangers can access personal conversations, photos, and other private information. Cybercriminals may use a loved ones' account to victimize friends/relatives that might not have known they passed.

Closing social media accounts after a family member's death may seem like a cold and impersonal task, but it is essential to address the emotional aspect of it. Social media has become a platform for people to express their thoughts, feelings, and memories. For the deceased, their social media accounts serve as a digital representation of their life. Therefore, it is essential to handle these accounts with sensitivity and respect. It is also crucial to highlight the importance of removing personal information and photos from the deceased's social media accounts. These accounts hold a wealth of personal data that should not be left unattended. Not only can it be used for malicious purposes, but it also goes against the deceased's right to privacy. Therefore, it is essential to take the necessary steps to protect their identity and reputation. Aside from the practical reasons for closing a deceased family member's social media account, there is also an emotional aspect to consider. Social media can be a way to keep memories alive, and the thought of permanently removing a loved one's online presence can be challenging to come to terms with. One way to preserve the deceased's digital memories is by creating a memorial page on the social media platform. This allows friends and family to continue sharing memories, stories, and messages to honor the deceased. Another option is to download photos and videos from the accounts and store them in a physical storage device, providing a tangible way to remember and cherish the deceased's online presence. This can be done by downloading photos and videos to a physical storage device, such as a USB drive or external hard drive. Search the social media platform's help section for how to download the account. This way, family members can keep and cherish these memories for years to come. Table 6.9 reflects things to consider when closing the deceased social media accounts.

TABLE 6.9 Considerations for Closing Social Media for the Deceased

Action		Description
1.	Choose a person to manage the process	The first step is to select a trusted family member or friend to handle the closure of the deceased's social media accounts. This person will need access to the accounts and should have a clear understanding of the deceased's wishes.
2.	Gather necessary information	Before starting the account closure process, it is essential to collect all the necessary information, including login credentials, email addresses associated with the accounts, and any other relevant details.
3.	Contact the social media platform	Each social media platform has its own process for closing accounts of deceased users. It is best to reach out to them directly and follow their specific instructions.
		Some platforms, such as Facebook, have a designated option for memorializing an account, where the profile is kept as a digital memorial for friends and family to remember the deceased.
4.	Provide necessary documents	Some social media platforms may require certain documents to verify the death, such as a death certificate or obituary. It is important to follow their instructions and provide the necessary documents to ensure the account is closed properly.
5.	Delete personal information	Once the accounts are closed, it is crucial to remove any personal information or photos of the deceased. This includes removing tags, posts, and comments that might contain sensitive information. It is also essential to check if the deceased had any other online accounts, such as email or online banking, and close them to prevent any potential identity theft.

The following list provides general steps for closing a loved one's accounts:

1. Log into the social media accounts using the provided credentials.

2. Go to the settings or account management section.

3. Look for an option to "deactivate" or "delete" the account.

4. If there is an option to deactivate, this will temporarily suspend the account and it can be reactivated later. If the user wants to permanently delete the account, look for an option to "delete" or "close" the account.

5. Follow the prompts and confirm the deletion of the account.

6. Repeat this process for all social media accounts belonging to the deceased.

Dealing with the passing of a loved ones passing can be terribly tough especially when dealing their personal social media which could include their private messaging. Table 6.10 has include some resources for dealing with the grief of the loved ones passing. We all handle grief differently. Don't be afraid to connect with these on-line or other local resources if you need to discuss the events.

TABLE 6.10 Online Resources Grief Support

Group	Description	Web address
GriefShare	Offers online grief support through video-based sessions, online resources, and an online grief support community.	https://www.griefshare.org
The Compassionate Friends	Provides a variety of online grief support resources, including chat rooms, virtual support groups, and online forums.	https://www.compassionatefriends.org
National Alliance for Grieving Children	Offers online support groups and webinars for children, teens, and their families who are grieving the loss of a loved one.	https://childrengrieve.org
Modern Loss	This online community offers support, resources, and personal essays for people who have experienced loss.	https://modernloss.com
Open to Hope	This Web site provides articles, podcasts, and videos on grief and loss, as well as an online community for support and connection.	https://www.opentohope.com

CONCLUSION

It is never too late to act and implement safety measures to protect our loved ones in the digital world. By being proactive and staying informed, we can create a safe and secure online environment for our adult family members. This can involve setting up privacy settings on social media accounts, using secure passwords, and regularly updating our devices and software. It is also important to have open and honest conversations with our family members about the potential dangers of the Internet and how to stay safe. With the right tools and knowledge, we can all play a role in protecting ourselves and our loved ones in the digital world.

There are many resources available for those looking to learn more about online safety and security. Government agencies, nonprofit organizations, and technology companies offer a variety of educational materials and support programs. Additionally, there are many online courses and tutorials available for those looking to improve their digital literacy. By taking advantage of these resources, we can continue to learn and adapt with technology, and in turn, better protect ourselves and our loved ones in the digital world. Make a commitment to stay informed, stay vigilant, and take necessary steps to ensure a safe and secure online experience for ourselves and our adult family members.

REFERENCES

U.S. Department of Justice
Office of Public Affairs. 2023. "Four Individuals Charged for Laundering Millions from Cryptocurrency Investment Scams." U.S. DOJ Press Release 23-1419, December 14, 2023. *https://www.justice.gov/opa/pr/four-individuals-charged-laundering-millions-cryptocurrency-investment-scams*
Federal Bureau of Investigation Internet Crime Complaint Center. 2024. "2023 IC3 Elder Fraud Annual Report." *https://www.ic3.gov/Media/PDF/AnnualReport/2023_IC3ElderFraudReport.pdf*
U.S. Attorney's Office, Eastern District of Missouri. 2024. "Four Accused of Nationwide Financial Scam Targeting Elderly." USAOEMO Press Release, February 15, 2024. *https://www.justice.gov/usao-edmo/pr/four-accused-nationwide-financial-scam-targeting-elderly*
U.S. Attorney's Office, District of Montana. 2024. "India-based computer-hacking scam that targeted elderly across the country and stole $150,000 from a Kalispell woman sends Indian national to prison for more than four years." USAOMT Press Release, February 14, 2024. *https://www.justice.gov/usao-mt/pr/india-based-computer-hacking-scam-targeted-elderly-across-country-and-stole-150000*

CHAPTER 7

SURVIVING IN THE ONLINE MARKETPLACE BARGAINING HUNTING IN THE TWENTY-FIRST CENTURY

It is human nature to look for bargains. Before the Internet, those bargains were often found by visiting garage and yards sales and attending auctions. The Internet changed that and the arrival of online markets, such as eBay, Craigslist, Facebook Marketplace, Next Door, Etsy, and many more, tapped into that need to find bargains. The cybercriminals took notice and developed methods to steal in those online venues. Neither sellers nor buyers are immune to these crimes. These crimes are not limited to stealing online. Some buyers and sellers have been killed, assaulted, and/or robbed when they moved the online transaction to a real-world meet to exchange goods. This chapter discusses online marketplace risk and how to minimize that risk.

THE TRADITIONAL MARKETPLACE

The sale of goods and services before the Internet marketplace was straightforward. The marketplace was firmly governed by *caveat emptor* (let the buyer beware.) Participants could physically inspect the goods and look one another in the eye. There could be overrepresentation, but a buyer could use their senses and their judgement and take those overrepresentations into account when making their offer to buy or simply walk away. A buyer at a yard/garage sale or auction took their purchase with them so failure to deliver cases didn't happen. Sellers could be ripped off if they accepted a bad check or counterfeit currency but again those cases would be rare. If a product turned out to be defective, they knew where to return it or who to go after to get a refund. In the United States the Federal Trade Commission and the Better Business Bureau could assist with a brick-and-mortar business that engaged in deceptive business practices.

Mail order transactions were ripe venues for many of the types of Internet fraudulent acts we see now, such as failure to deliver, failure to pay, and bait and switch schemes. They again were tied to elements, such as addresses, mailboxes, etc. that could be used to track down the fraudsters. The U.S. Postal Service has years of experience in shutting down these fraudsters. There were sophisticated fraudsters that would find ways to make tracking them difficult but nothing like what is seen with online fraud criminals. The Internet created opportunities not only for the novice fraudster but the sophisticated fraudsters and organizations to excel.

THE INTERNET MARKETPLACE

The Internet drastically changed how goods are bought and sold. No longer do sellers and buyers need to be geographically close. Traditional garage/yard and auctions had fixed locations and set times for sales to occur. Internet markets don't sleep and are not bound by these limitations. This is a perfect environment for a fraudster to operate. Distance between them and their victims makes prosecution more difficult. The ability for fraudsters to conceal their real identity and their true location can't be accomplished to such an extent in the brick-and-mortar world. The ability to quickly *shut down* and move their online operation can be done in minutes. Digital images of products can easily be created without the fraudster even possessing them. Their fictitious inventory can easily be stored and moved as needed. Electronic financial transactions open new avenues for fraud that can't occur when the buyer and seller are dealing in cash transactions face to face.

Common Internet Fraud

There are at least seven cybercrime methods for profiting from Internet fraud. They are:

1. *Nondelivery of Merchandise/ Nondelivery of Payment:* One of the most common fraud methods is failure of the seller to deliver the goods or for the buyer to fail to make payment.

2. *Bait and Switch:* This occurs when the fraudulent seller represents one product for sale but delivers a substandard or defective product.

3. *Overpayment Fraud:* The fraudulent buyer *inadvertently* overpays for an item and requests an overpayment refund. The problem is the entire payment was a fake. The seller refunds the overpayment only to learn that the fraudulent buyer reversed their original payment in full or the original check paid was no good. To make matters worse, if the seller also sent the item, they are out not only their product but the *overpayment*.

4. *Triangulation Fraud:* An unsuspecting buyer places an order using credit, debit, or some other electronic method with a fraudulent seller. The fraudulent seller takes the funds from the unsuspecting buyer but uses stolen credit information to purchase the item for the buyer, using the buyer's billing details as a delivery address. The buyer doesn't realize that the fraudulent seller used stolen credit card information to fill their order.

5. *Identify Theft:* The *seller* (fraudster) may or may not be interested in selling anything. Their goals are to get credit cards and personal information for later committing identify theft or to facilitate triangulation fraud.

6. *Fraudulent Additional Purchases:* The buyer purchases one product or service only to later realize the seller also used their credit card information to buy additional items or services that they did not agree to buy. Sometimes these additional charges will appear weeks or months later with goods or services delivered or not delivered. This is common in vitamin and supplement markets.

7. *Account Takeovers:* Cybercriminals obtain access to legitimate seller and buyer accounts. They then use these stolen accounts to commit the frauds previously listed or sell saved card details, payment gateway, and digital wallet accounts if available.

Common Methods to Further Internet Fraud

Online criminals can use many methods to lure an unsuspecting victim into believing the online scheme is real. Methods can include digital images (often copied from a real Web site) of nonexistent products in their posts. Other methods of misdirection can be a bit more sophisticated, and they often can include:

1. *Fake Reviews:* Fraudsters have a variety of methods to build up their credibility to make themselves look legitimate. These include using bots which are operated by other cybercriminals to post favorable reviews.

2. *Account Collusion:* Fraudulent sellers will set up fake buyer/seller accounts to vouch for their fraudulent accounts. This adds to their creditability by manipulating their ratings. They will so use fake transactions between the accounts to avoid scrutiny.

3. *Bid Shielding/Shilling:* In an Internet auction criminals will use fake accounts to drive up bids to secure more profits for the fraudulent seller. In bid shilling a buyer with a partner or fake account will artificially inflate the bids, discouraging others from bidding. At the last minute, the shilling account cancels the high bid and permits the fraudulent buyer to win the auction with a lower bid.

PROTECTION METHODS IN ONLINE MARKETS

Caveat emptor (let the buyer/seller beware) is just as true in online markets as it is in traditional markets. Don't rely on just appearances of digital images of products, buyer/seller profiles and reviews. If the sale price or product presented is too good to be true it likely is. Complete some due diligence Internet research on the buyer or seller as well as the product being offered for sale. Use not only their names and profiles but email addresses and telephone numbers, and mail addresses they provide in conducting that research. There could already be reports online about problems with them. A relatively new profile may be a concern. Numerous reviews with similar or the same comments may be an indication that they are fake. Avoid sellers without contact information or who refuse to provide legitimate contact information. Additionally, take the following steps:

Table 7.1 Online Transactions Security Checklist has been provided to give you an easy to use checklist to assist with your security in online transactions.

1. *Get the seller/buyer to provide a phone number and verify it.*
    a. Be cautious of numbers that are connected for services like Google Voice. There are reports where scammers will try to *verify* a user's identity by sending a text message with a Google Voice verification code and ask the user for that code. If the user gives them the verification code, they'll try to use it to create a Google Voice number linked to the user's phone number which they will use for fraudulent transactions.
    b. Does the voice connected to the number match who they claim to be from? For instance, if the person claims they are from one location, but they speak in a manner inconsistent with their whereabouts, such as with a foreign accent or broken English, that is a red flag.
    c. Do they only speak to the user at a time of their choosing? This may be an indication they are using a cohort that sounds more legitimate to communicate with the user. Someone without an accent may sound more convincing. They may also be more sophisticated in getting the sales closed. The same applies to video calls. They may be using a cohort that presents a better presence to look more convincing.
    d. Be aware of telephone calls where the clarity is bad. This may be an indication that the call is being made from a foreign location via the Internet. It also makes it difficult to ascertain the voice and legitimacy of the caller.

2. *Forms of Payment:* Beware of buyers who insist on wire transfers as the only form of payment they'll accept. A common scheme is to overpay and then retrieve the entire payment after the user returns the overpayment. Similarly, do not cash checks that are an overpayment. Don't cash the check but instead ask for a check

in the exact purchase price. Again, it is a common scheme to provide a bad check as an overpayment and get the seller to return the overage. If given a cashier's check, money order or other equivalent, call the bank at a number the user finds online, not a number provided by the buyer, to verify the check's validity.

3. *Escrow Services:* For big-ticket items, use a legitimate online escrow service that will hold the payment until the buyer receives what they've ordered.

4. *Never Provide a Social Security or Driver's License Number:* Legitimate sellers don't ask for that information, but an identity thief would.

5. *Use a Credit Card to Make Online Purchases:* This provides added protection through the credit card company if the goods are not provided or are defective. Additionally, many credit cards will alert the user when an attempt to purchase from a vendor that has a history of fraudulent transactions and stop the transaction from going through.

6. *In-Person Transactions:* At times the seller and buyer will complete the transaction in person. This substantially increases the possible risk of not only financial but physical harm. Arrange the meeting place in a public place, specifically a police station or property. Criminals want nothing to do with the police and will avoid meeting at such a location. Besides a police presence they also usually have cameras monitoring the area, a further deterrence to those criminally inclined. Inside the police station is best if possible. Many police stations have established Internet Sales Safe Zone, or Safe Trade Zones (See Table 7.2 In Person exchange of goods) specifically to make buyers and sellers safe during these transactions. Safe Trade Stations (*https://www.safetradestations.com/safetrade-station-list.html*) has a listing of police agencies providing this service. If the meeting location does not have a participating police agency, contact the local police, and discuss the need for a safe place to facilitate the transaction. They will advise accordingly of hours of operation and further specifics.

Online Research of Telephone Numbers

Looking up a telephone number can reveal information on the owner. A simple Google search can reveal quite a bit, particularly if it has been reported as a contact in fraudulent schemes. There are also numerous sites online that let a user add the number and research databases to provide information on the number and its owner. Some sites charge a nominal fee for the search information. Here are a few such sites:

■ *https://www.intelius.com/reverse-phone-lookup/*

■ *https://socialcatfish.com/reverse-phone-lookup/*

■ *https://www.peoplelooker.com/*

Be aware that the information provided may not always be accurate and they might provide information on the wrong person.

Investigate the Merchant Before Buying

Users want to believe that what is seen in an ad on Facebook or somewhere else on the Internet is a legitimate vendor looking for business. This is simply not the case. Online criminals work hard to fool users into thinking they are real. Reviewing the merchant's Web site, looking for reviews and sampling Googling may prevent the user from making a regretful online transaction. Start by going directly to their Web site. Look through the Web site especially at their "About" page and the links that may appear at the bottom of the page. These can be linked to other Web sites and can reveal information of interest about the site's ownership. Look up the merchant's name on the Better Business Bureau's Web site. Are they even listed; are there complaints? Research other buyer's reviews on social media, blogs and scam reporting sites like Scam Advisor (*https://www.scamadviser.com/*) to identify complaints about the merchant.

IDENTIFYING FRAUDULENT WEB SITES

A simple way to identify if a Web site is a scam site is to copy and paste the site address (URL) into one of several Web sites, all of which have their own database of problem Web sites. Consider checking with more than one of the following Web sites:

- *https://www.scamadviser.com/*
- *https://www.urlvoid.com/*
- *https://www.lookout.com/life/free-online-shopping-checker*
- *https://www.scamdoc.com/*

Vendors Using Social Media Accounts

Some vendors are only selling through social media accounts. These require research as well. How recently was the account created? Can the person who created the account be identified? Does the social media account provide contact information, such as telephone numbers, emails, and/or a mailing address? This information all needs to be confirmed. Check for buyer/seller reviews on the social media site. If anything looks questionable avoid transactions with this vendor.

DANGERS USING PERSONAL DEBIT/CREDIT CARDS

Online debit cards and credit cards are two different things. They end up using the same credit transaction system, but they are legally different and the user's personal liability and the bank's requirement to replace the funds may be different. A debit card is like a modern check transaction. It is a debit against funds the user actually has in their account. A credit card is an extension of credit and is the banking institution's money. Depending on the circumstances of the fraud encountered the bank may not be as quick to replace personal funds as it will be to deal with a loss on credit that was provided. Debit cards have better security than in the past. There is still the possibility a fraudster can access their bank account through a debit card and drain personal funds. Using a credit card to make online purchases is most often the best security option.

Third-Party Wallets or Virtual Cards

A good way to help prevent fraud when making purchases online is to use a third party wallet which is available if the user has an account with Google, Apple, or PayPal. They have a payment system that can be used to protect the user's transactions. They use a process called *tokenization*. They provide a virtual credit card number or payment through their system and not the user's original card.

Many credit card companies offer virtualized cards as an option. Privacy.com (*https://privacy.com/*) also offers a service of virtual cards numbers to help prevent the user from becoming a victim.

Report Problems Immediately

Report any unauthorized transactions on debit/credit card immediately. This should be to the banking institution and law enforcement. The sooner the report is made the sooner the funds can be returned to the user's account. Law enforcement will generally provide a case number which the bank may want as proof the crime has been reported.

TABLE 7.1 Online Transactions Security Checklist

Item to check	Action	Verified
Regularly check your credit/debit accounts	Check account activity regularly. Is there a transaction that was not authorized? Contact the bank if something unusual or questionable is detected.	
Credit/debit card PIN protection	Do not give a personal identification number to anyone strangers, family members or any caller.	
Avoid public networks	Public Internet networks (coffee shops, airports, and other public places) are not secure. If a user must use one consider the use of a VPN to prevent eaves dropping.	

Item to check	Action	Verified
Strong passwords	Again, strong passwords especially on financial and banking information is critical to preventing becoming a victim of a crime.	
Use secure Web sites	Look for the little *lock* feature on the Web sites. This means they are secure. Make sure to look for it before entering debit or credit details. If it is not present stop entering information.	
Look for phishing attacks	Phishing can take the form of a fake Web site or account login page that appears to be legitimate but is not. Blindly following links in an email, text message or even from a Web page can be dangerous.	
Two-factor authentication (2FA)	Ensure two-factor authentication is set for banking information.	
Account alerts	Setup up account alerts for transactions of any kind to notify when something is transacted on the user's account.	

TABLE 7.2 In Person Exchanges of Goods

1.	Police provide their presence to make sure everyone is safe. Departments will have rules about onsite exchanges, such as specific hours of availability, appointments required, and no firearms. If possible, have the meeting inside the department.
2.	Meet only during daylight hours unless the police department has offered inside facilities twenty-four hours a day.
3.	Police will not get involved in the transaction details. If the item being exchanged might be stolen some police departments may be willing to check the serial number of a sale item to determine if it's in a database of stolen property.
4.	Be careful carrying a large sum of cash, either before or after the transaction. Take precautions to protect against being followed when the transaction is completed. Follow this chapter's precautions on accepting checks or other payment forms.

Some items are impractical to meet at a police station for exchanges, such as large furniture or a vehicle that isn't running. The following is therefore suggested:

- If the transaction must occur outside the police station, there is safety in numbers. Never be outnumbered. Have two or more other individuals there and make sure the other party knows that others will be present.

- Never let someone go anywhere unaccompanied in one's home, not even to the bathroom. Always make sure they are escorted.

- Don't have more than one group come to the user's residence at one time to buy or sell.

CONCLUSION

This chapter has provided an overview of best practices for securing purchases online. This includes a checklist of things to consider when purchasing items online and some resources to help prevent the user from having their credit or debit card compromised. Chapter 8 will discuss small business protection.

PROTECTING A SMALL HOME BUSINESS

IN THIS CHAPTER

This chapter discusses concepts of small home business (SHB) protection. Topics include prevention methods from business scams, handling social media as an SHB, backing up data, data destruction for out-of-date systems, Acceptable Use Policy, and monitoring SHB employees' computer use.

SHB IN THE TWENTY-FIRST CENTURY

Commerce changed as the result of the coronavirus pandemic. SHB owners who did not think they needed an online presence faced the harsh reality of trying to survive in a world where social distancing became the new norm. The new model, even for traditional *brick and mortar* businesses like restaurants, requires them to embrace having a robust online presence. Retail businesses have to offer the ability for customers to shop and buy online. Before coronavirus, many businesses permitted employees the flexibility to telework. Those who did not embrace teleworking are now seeing it as a necessity to continue operations during chaotic times.

Creating an online presence also makes businesses, their employees, and their customers all potential targets for criminals. During the pandemic, criminals did not practice distancing for their illegal behavior, including disrupting Zoom meetings. The issues covered earlier in the book for personal cybersecurity are obviously applicable to SHBs. Create a Digital Risk Checklist for SHB computers as reflected in Table 2.4. This will be important in case hardware is lost or stolen. Continue to refer to those particular chapters as needed to cover SHB cyberprotection. This chapter covers additional areas that are somewhat unique to an SHB.

PREVENTING COMMON BUSINESS SCAMS

Today's business scams attack by email or telephone call. Their success depends upon the owner's or SHB employee's naïveté about technology. Prevention is possible by implementing good practices. A lapse of good practice can result in a terrible situation, such as the ransomware encryption of all of an SHB's data.

Common Scams that Target Small Businesses

The Federal Trade Commission [2024] identifies nine small business scams that are a variation of fraudulent schemes noted elsewhere in this book. They are:

Fake Invoices and Unordered Merchandise

Phony invoices are sometimes sent to an SHB. They mirror products or services an SHB might order. The fraudsters are counting on the person responsible for paying expenses assuming they are legitimate and making payment. Scammers also will call an SHB to confirm a fictitious order by verifying an address or offering a free catalog or sample. If the SHB answers yes to any of the scammer's inquiries the unordered merchandise will arrive at the SHB. This is then followed by the scammers' high-pressure demands for payment. Remember in the United States any unordered merchandise received can be kept without making payment. Figure 8.1 is an example of what a phishing email and attachment could look like. Be aware of the kinds of phishing attempts that are occurring and don't click on emails or their attachments without knowing for sure that they are real and not from a scammer.

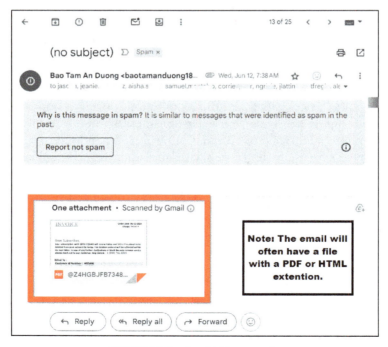

FIGURE 8.1 Invoice phishing example.

Online Listing and Advertising Scams

Scammers will also try to trick SHB into paying for nonexistent advertising or a listing in a phony business directory. They will again use tactics to get confirmation from the SHB. Later, the SHB will get a big bill, and the scammer may use details from their previous interaction or even a recording to pressure payment.

Business and Government Impersonation Scams

SHBs are not immune to this scam. A scammer pretending to be a trusted entity will try to scare an SHB into rushing payment or giving information. They will pretend to be a utility company threatening to shut off services that will interrupt business operations. Some scammers will claim they are a Web hosting company and will threaten the SHB will lose their Web site URL if payment is not immediately. Pretending to be government agents, they will threaten to suspend business licenses, impose fines, or initiate civil action. Some will try to sell workplace compliance posters that a SHM can get for free. Others will try to convince s SHB to pay an application fee for a nonexistent business grant.

Tech Support Scams

Tech support scams also target SHBs. The goal is to get access to money or computer systems, or both. The scammer claims to an unsuspecting employee that they are an SHB's tech support and they need access to help with an update or some other nonexistent problem. Once gaining access scammers will go after an SHB's sensitive data like passwords, customer records, or credit card information.

Social Engineering, Phishing, and Ransomware

Cyberscammers will trick employees into believing they are a supervisor or senior employee to get them into sending money or giving confidential or sensitive information like passwords or bank information. It can start with a phishing email, social media contact, or a call and will stress the need for urgency in providing the information. Scammers will use spear phishing tactics to send targeted emails to specific employees to gain access. Malicious emails are used to trick an employee into clicking on a link that infects their system or encrypts data which can only be unencrypted by payment of a fee to the scammer.

Business Coaching Scams

Some scammers will con SHBs with bogus business coaching programs. The programs use false testimonials, videos, seminar presentations, and telemarketing calls and promise to help grow the SHB. They may start with low initial costs that only grow with more services offered. The growth promises never materialize.

Changing Online Reviews

Some scammers will claim to post online reviews to help an SHB for a small fee. Others may threaten to post unfavorable online reviews unless payment is made. Posting fake reviews is illegal.

Credit Card Processing and Equipment Leasing Scams

Scammers know SHBs are looking to cut costs. Under this scam, they promise lower rates for processing credit card transactions or better deals on equipment leasing. They scammers will fail to deliver on these promises and are only interested in getting the SHB's money.

Fake Check Scams

The overpayment scam has been discussed before. In this case the scammer is targeting an SHB with a check that exceeds what was due. They convince the SHB to send the overpayment back. The scammer's original check later bounces leaving the SHB out the cost of the payment they sent the scammer.

Instituting Best Practices

Even the smallest of businesses should have some documentation on what acceptable practices are. To prevent mishaps, all employees should receive initial and regular periodic training on those acceptable practices. Table 8.1 provides a checklist of acceptable practices.

TABLE 8.1 Scam Prevention Checklist

Action	Date
Train employees to prevent fraud.	
Verify invoices and payments and segregate accounting duties.	
Maintain internal controls.	
Know employees. Check references and do employee background checks.	
Be tech-savvy: Learn about the technology the SHB uses.	
Protect client credit card information and any personal identifiers collected.	
Limit staff access to data, including the ability to modify it. Employees should only have access to data needed to perform their job function. More than one embezzlement has occurred when a thief adds a fictitious vendor to a system to get checks fraudulently issued, which they later cash.	
Consider purchasing insurance to mitigate fraud losses.	
Report scams to the FTC or local law enforcement.	

Free and Low-Cost Online Cybersecurity Learning Content

SHB owners and their employees need to keep regularly informed on cybersecurity issues. Employee awareness training is available from the National Institute of Standards and Training program, the National Initiative for Cybersecurity Education (NICE) *https://www.nist.gov/itl/applied-cybersecurity/nice/resources/ online-learning-content*. The links on the Web site are for free or low-cost online educational training. The topics range from information technology to cybersecurity. Consider using these Web sites as a regular cybersecurity education program.

Acceptable Use Policy (AUP)

Human beings are frequently the weakness link in computer security. Either through error or intentional acts they annually cause significant employer losses. SHBs need an acceptable use policy (AUP) that establishes what employees are allowed to do with their computer resources to prevent harm to business systems and data. Examples of harm include destruction of data/systems, theft of intellectual property, and fraud. Another example is loss of productivity as employees are wasting time on computer resources playing games, surfing the Internet, or working on nonbusiness-related tasks. Employees can also use SHB computers to engage in sexual harassment behavior (viewing and sharing porn and sending explicit messages with other employees) or sending harassing and threatening messages.

A proper AUP will spell out what is acceptable and unacceptable conduct and provides a mechanism to compel compliance, including penalties for noncompliance. AUPs also alert employees that they have no expectation of privacy when using employer owned equipment allowing employers to monitor and log their computer behavior. Along with a written AUP, computers users should see a banner when they start up or log on to an employer computer. AUP also should cover *bring your own devices* (BYOD) when those devices are used for business purposes. An AUP should also cover an employee's social media use if it impacts the SHB. A simple Google search can provide an AUP that an SHB can modify to meet their needs.

Enforcing AUP

The first component to enforcing an AUP is to establish which computer a user is authorized to use. This can be a device specifically assigned to them or a computer with several different user profiles which have been set up for their use. SHB may need to outsource setting up user profiles depending upon their personnel's level of expertise.

SHBs should document the specific device or user account associated with each employee. SHB should also assign employees a specific email account for them if their job function requires it. Once an SHB has designated a device or user account it can then establish which employer system components/services an employee can access. This can be accomplished in a number of ways. When setting up user accounts, the SHB can restrict which programs they run, whether they can install software/hardware, or what files they can access. An SHB can even limit the hours employees have for Internet access. An SHB can also accomplish restrictions through specific programs and by using the business router.

The final component is monitoring employee compliance with the AUP. This can be accomplished by file activity monitoring (FAM). There are free and paid programs that perform FAM. It is suggested conducting a Google search to find the best one suited to an SHB's needs. There are also YouTube videos that show how to deploy and use FAM. A good feature to look for in a FAM is the ability to send alerts. An important alert to consider are attempts to access/copy/remove sensitive files/folders. Others are alerts on hits by antivirus software.

Beyond FAM there are monitoring software programs that will record key-strokes typed and take screen shots of user's activities. As noted in Chapter 5, there can be legal implications for deploying such software. An additional consideration is these programs can store user activity logs. A Google search can locate the top current monitoring programs that best suits an SHB's needs. Any violations of an AUB detected should be investigated and addressed promptly.

BUSINESS SOCIAL MEDIA

All the precautions discussed in the previous chapters mentioning social media are just as valid for businesses as well. Table 8.2 lists some additional considerations for businesses having a social media presence.

TABLE 8.2 Business Social Media Checklist

Action	Date
Plan how the SHB wants to use social media and which sites are appropriate to further the business.	
Open a social media account consistent with a site's requirements for businesses. Some social media sites have features that are specific to businesses. For instance, Facebook has both business pages, which represent a business or brand, and personal pages, which are for individuals. Individuals are not supposed to set up an account for a business as if they were an individual.	
Review the site's features specific to business accounts, such as controls for restricting posts/comments, moderation of posts, procedures for granting access to users, granting control to moderators, etc.	
Consider how much to allow customers/clients to interact with the business's social media. Can they post comments? If comments are allowed, consider using the moderation controls that may be present on a particular social media site.	
Consider how each post fits with the SHB's overall marketing plan. If it doesn't fit, don't post it.	
Define which employee(s) will have access to social media to make posts, moderate other's posts, and respond to posts.	
Consider how the SHB is going to monitor the account. Can the SHB give an employee this ability and if so, who?	
Document accounts and passwords consistent with Chapter 4 Table 4.1 and require staff not to change passwords without management approval.	

CONFERENCING SECURITY BEST PRACTICES

During the coronavirus pandemic conferencing was quite common as were disruptions by uninvited guests. Here are some considerations to conducting online conference meetings:

Attendees

Know how to operate the software prior to the meeting. Some tools like Microsoft Teams have many features that users might not initially understand and finding out how they function during the first online meeting is not a good idea. Know the features before starting live. Setting up the software before the meeting starts may be required, since waiting for the conference start time may put the user behind and late for the meeting. Is video needed to be on during the meeting? What is in the video background that can be used to identify the user or their location? While in the meeting, act like the microphone and camera are always on, even if they are muted and/or off. This will prevent the user from saying or doing something improper in the event the microphone and/or camera becomes unmuted.

Host

Open meetings can allow unwanted people to attend. Make sure to create a meeting ID and a password that is given just to the meeting attendees. If the meeting software has a lock feature, lock the meeting after everyone has accessed the meeting room. This helps to prevent any possible intruders from gaining access. Consider whether to record the meeting and the legal issues associated with recording them. If recording the meeting, make sure everyone is informed that the meeting is being recorded before starting. (See Chapter 5, Legal Issues) When the meeting is over, don't share the link to the video unless it's appropriate. Once sent to someone else, the user has no control over the link unless it is secured with a username and password access.

Use the virtual waiting room feature for the meetings to allow people to join, and don't start the meeting until it is ready. Consider not allowing screen sharing unless it is limited to a few participants. Does the meeting need video for the participants? Consider just using the audio. Also consider whether the chat or instant message feature is on during the meeting and if someone needs to address those messages in real time during the meeting.

DATA BACK UPS ARE AN SHB NECESSITY

Data loss happens all the time. Sometimes it's accidental, and sometimes it is not. Data retention is critical to the SHB's continued operation. Every essential computer that operates in the business needs to have a backup plan. This is not only for the fear of a virus or ransomware, but also for things like floods, fire, and so on. Hard drives, even the solid-state variety, fail. Spending a few hundred dollars up-front will save the SHB spending thousands later on recovery costs.

Making a Data Backup Plan

Businesses come in a variety of sizes. If the user's SHB approaches significant size, consider speaking with an accountant and/or lawyer about what records need to be backed up and the best method for doing so. This discussion here is intended for the smallest of businesses, with significantly fewer employees and/or revenue. The SHB may wish to consider outsourcing their data storage and IT needs depending upon their size.

Identify Important Data

Identify what data is critical to the SHB. Common SHB examples are any records that reflect income received, expected income (accounts receivable), paid expenses, expenses needing paid (accounts payable), sales receipts, and assets, such as inventory. Any information pertaining to suppliers and customers is also important. Depending on the business's size, these records may be maintained in accounting files or spreadsheets. Records in word-processing documents, such as templates for invoices and letterheads, business plans/reports, personnel records, and draft contracts are also important. Other records may be scanned, such as signed contracts and tax returns. Some records may be emails to or from suppliers and customers. Other records might be digital inventory photos.

The next consideration is identifying all the devices that deal with this kind of data. These would obviously include desktop or laptop computers but might also include mobile devices as well. If the SHB has a network, is the data maintained on a network server on a user's computer or both. After identifying the devices, consider how many kinds of important data is maintained on the device. It may make sense to back up only particular drives/folders of a device, or it might make sense to back up the entire device's storage. Table 8.3 provides considerations for data backup. This is not an all-inclusive list but covers much of the important data an SHB needs backed up. Review the SHB's data and identify where the data is normally stored to properly complete this list.

TABLE 8.3 Critical Data Types to Consider Backing Up

Action	Date
Company Personnel Records	
Federal, state, and local tax records	
Payroll records	
Pension/401K records	
Current and past employee records	
Administrative Documents	
Sales data	
Marketing data	
Social media account information	
Insurance records	
Leasing documents for equipment and property	
Attorney/client material	
Pending legal case information	
Federal and state tax filings	

Action	Date
Financial Data	
Finance system data	
Daily transactions	
Web site transactions	
Equipment inventory	
Revenue records	
Bank statements	
Expense receipts	
Travel receipts	
Proprietary Data	
Customer lists	
Sales data	
Trademark and patent filings	
Proprietary code	

Storage Needs/Cost

An SHB has identified its critical data and where it is maintained. Now it needs to decide how often data needs backed up, what is the best backup solution for the SHB (software/hardware/cloud), and what it is going to cost. Figure 8.2 describes the basic data storage concepts typically available to a home user.

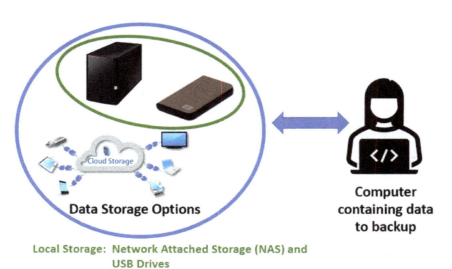

FIGURE 8.2 Data storage options

Cloud Storage

Many business applications are available through cloud technology, which is just another form of backup. Evaluate in the SHB plan how much data is stored in the cloud and how data can be accessed after an incident. Using online backup services makes backing up all data simple. The lesson learned, however, is that this needs to be managed. If an SHB is using cloud backups, when was the last time it checked the cloud services files to ensure that the data is being backed up, and is it the current version of an SHB's data? Did someone working on the bookkeeping system make a new personnel folder that is not in the cloud backup plan? If so, those necessary files might not have been backed up.

Local Data Backups

Is the SHB saving files to an attached USB Drive? This can simplify the backup process if all the necessary files are copied to a second drive installed on an SHB's computer. Choosing a system for locally backing up an SHB's data can be cost effective, but it has issues that need to be considered. What is the backup schedule? The best practice for an SHB would be to back up nightly. Backup software programs for individuals and SHBs are readily available. Most allow users to set a schedule that will automatically back up their data at regular times each day or night. Software that has encryption can increase data security, preventing hackers from having access and stopping the release of an SHB's client's personal data.

Recent backup copies should be removed from the premises and stored off-site. If the office burns down the business can survive the tragedy if the backups are safe off-site. None of this works if the SHB does not adhere to the backup schedule and the removal of the copies to off-site storage.

Using a Network Attached Storage Device

A network attached storage device (NAS) is a very effective method for backing up data for an SHB. A NAS is a file-level data storage server connected to the SHB network. The beauty of these small devices is that they can provide computer data storage to everyone across a network. A NAS can be attached to the internal company router and provide a separate drive letter for everyone to back up their data. Most of them are simple devices to install and operate and don't need an IT person to install them. Since they are still hard drives, they need to be monitored. They are a great option for backups and data retention. In Figure 8.3 we have described could properly backup their data to prevent data loss. Following this process helps the home user to secure their data in multiple locations, thereby preventing the loss from having data stored in a single location.

Best Small Home Business Data Backup Concept

Computer containing data to backup	Local USB Drive or NAS containing data	USB Drive containing data Stored offsite	Cloud Service containing data
1	2	3	4

FIGURE 8.3 Best SHB data backup concept.

DISPOSING OF SHB EQUIPMENT

Backing up is important, but what does an SHB do with all their business computers and cell phones when no longer needed? Does an SHB need to retain the data for legal purposes? Does the SHB have a policy for data retention? Is it consistent with the law?

A primary consideration for disposing equipment is not to allow any personal, company, or client data to remain on the devices. Donating SHB equipment to a nonprofit that repairs and reintroduces the equipment to people who need it is a good thing. If an SHB's client data remains on the device that creates a big security issue. Here are some things to consider when disposing of SHB equipment.

The number one goal is to make your business data unreadable. The data destruction should ensure that no person can recover any data. It's important to consider the time involved in the process as well as the cost. Another consideration is the destruction required under a legal requirement. If it is, make sure the destruction process complies with the laws the SHB may be required to satisfy. One of the best standards for data destruction is the National Institute of Standards and Technology (NIST) guidelines (*https://nvlpubs.nist.gov/nistpubs/specialpublications/nist.sp.800-88r1.pdf*). Here are some possible data destruction methods:

1. *Delete/reformat:* This is the least recommended process, as the data can potentially be recovered.

2. *Data wiping:* This is the process of writing data over the existing data to obliterate the existing data completely.

3. *Degaussing:* This is the process of using high-powered magnets to destroy the data (this may work on a hard drive but not on solid-state devices).

4. *Physical destruction:* Destruction of the device by drilling holes into a hard drive, using a hammer to break the device into pieces, or shredding. There are hard drive shredders made for complete drive destruction.

These techniques can be used on computers, hard drives, cellphones, thumb drives, or an IOT device. An SHB's destructive choice is based on the time and costs involved in the process. Another potential resource is finding a local company specializing in data destruction.

Data Retention Legal Requirements

Has the SHB been told that they need to retain data for a lawsuit? Reacting timely and appropriately is a necessity to avoid costly litigation expenses, including court sanctions. Data can easily be overwritten and an SHB can be blamed for the loss even if it is unintentional. Contact an attorney and a digital forensic specialist for data retention advice and assistance as soon as possible.

Device Tracking

There are programs that can help SHB keep track of their devices in case they are stolen or lost. They frequently also can remotely wipe the device to prevent data theft. Again, a Google search is one of the best ways to find the product that fits the SHB's needs.

CONCLUSION

This chapter has provided an overview of best practices for SHB to protect their systems and data. These practices include educating staff and establishing use polices, including on social media. Various methods were covered for backing up data as well as securing destroying it when it is no longer needed. Chapter 9 will discuss surviving a cyberattack.

REFERENCES

Federal Trade Commission. 2024. "Scams and Your Small Business: A Guide for Business." Federal Trade Commission, July 2024. *https://www.ftc.gov/business-guidance/resources/scams-your-small-business-guide-business#comm onscams*

CHAPTER 9

SURVIVING A DIGITAL (CYBER) ATTACK

IN THIS CHAPTER

This chapter discusses how to prevent, survive, and respond to specific cyber-attack and stresses steps covered in previous chapters.

SURVIVING A CYBERATTACK

A cyber-attack was considered a disruption or theft of equipment or data. The term has expanded to include attacks that impact a person beyond just their data or equipment, such as cyberstalking, someone posting illicit images of a former lover (revenge porn), or doxing, the release of personal information, such as your address and telephone number on a social media site for harassment purposes. Cyberattacks also include computer use to sexually exploit children and the emotionally/mentally vulnerable. They occur in different ways. (See Figure 9.1). The attacker may try to gain access to your device to steal data or plant malware to encrypt data for ransom. In the case of a cyber-stalker, they may have been able to insert spyware on the user's system to track their online and offline activities. In other cases, such as cyberbullying, they may harass the user or their loved ones online without direct access to the user's data or system. They frequently attack the most vulnerable, our kids and older loved ones. Being able to survive any of these requires some planning and levelheaded responses. There are many types of potential cyberattacks that can harm, disable, or steal data. Some of the common attacks and ways to prevent them are referenced in Table 9.1.

Common Cyber Threats

Identity Theft

Malware

Ransomware

Trojan

Phishing

FIGURE 9.1 Common cyberthreats.

TABLE 9.1 Attacks and prevention.

Attacks	Prevention
Malware: A malicious file that is downloaded to a computer. The file can potentially steal credit card data, collect user keystrokes and passwords, and/or encrypt the device data and demand ransom. This all depends on the software's preprogrammed functionality. *Trojan horse:* A Trojan, or Trojan horse, is malware that delivers its payload by hiding itself within something legitimate. This can be a software download update from a malicious site or possibly a link in an email or a legitimate-looking attachment that contains the malware. *Ransomware:* A malware program specifically designed to encrypt the files on a user's computer and present a demand for a ransom to receive the decryption key. The hacker wants payment in a crypto currency at a specific Web site generally hidden on the Dark Web.	1. Avoid downloading programs or executables from unrecognized vendors or those that attempt to alarm the user to a serious problem. Don't click on links in an email or in a text message. Get in the habit of scanning attachments sent from known sources before opening them. Do not accept USB devices unless you know the source and still scan them. 2. Have an up-to-date antivirus program installed on all devices. 3. Backup all data. (See Chapter 8 for suggestions).
Social Engineering: The manipulation of people into performing actions or divulging confidential information. Social engineering is the art of psychological manipulation. The manipulation goal is to get the victim to give up confidential information or to trick them into taking some action. Criminals use these methods because it can be easier to exploit a user's natural desire to trust than to attempt a system exploit. Social engineering can be personal, such as via a telephone call, or impersonal through letters or electronic communication (emails, or text messages). Phishing/spear phishing/ smishing are forms of social engineering involving electronic communication.	4. No one should ask for a user's password, username, or social security number over the phone. Never give out personal information to people you don't know, no matter how nice they seem. 5. Do not honor requests for systems information from someone the users doesn't know. Additionally, do not follow their instructions to go to a site or take some action on the user's system. 6. Don't click on links in an email or in a text message. If needed go to the site, by opening a browser and going directly to the site to prevent phishing.

Attacks	Prevention
Cyberstalking/Cyberharassment is the use of the Internet or other electronic means to harass, intimidate, or frighten someone. This includes both children and adults. This can include someone posting illicit images of a former lover (revenge porn) or doxing, the release of personal information, such as your address and telephone number, on a social media site for harassment purposes.	7. Limit the amount of personal information published online. Sharing too much gives the stalker more information to use against the victim. It is common for a stalker to access a victim's accounts and to gain information that can be used to threaten or blackmail them. 8. Check the privacy settings on all of accounts. Many social media and other tools require users to make security and privacy changes themselves. These are not automatic changes. 9. Turn on two-factor authentication previously discussed in this book.

Phishing, Spear Phishing, and Smishing

A phishing scam is an official-looking email from the government, a bank, or a well-known company that cons the victim into exposing their system. The email may contain a link or other instructions to follow that trick the victim into providing the attacker with personal or company information such as banking details or login and password information for accounts. Phishing attacks frequently involve sending hundreds or thousands of emails to users purporting to be from a specific bank or company, with the random hope that some of their targets actually have a relationship with the entity they are purporting to be from. Spear phishing uses the same techniques, but it is a targeted attack, usually toward a business or government agency. They will purport to be an entity that the intended target will trust. For instance, they will create an email purporting to be from inside a target's employer, such as a president, to convince the target to take some action that is detrimental to the employer. The action sought varies but could include allowing the attacker to gain access to the employer's systems or to convince them to wire transfer funds outside the employer. Smishing is the same as phishing but is accomplished via sending text messages instead of emails. Figure 9.2 is an example of another phishing emails using known companies that the receiver might actual have as a service. It is necessary in today's email security to review any emails you receive especially if they come from a known service. The scammers copy a known service and intentionally use the same messages and images to attempt to fool you into clicking on the emails and then using your login and password to gain access to the account. Unfortunately that website is the scammers and you just gave them your username and password which they can use take over your account.

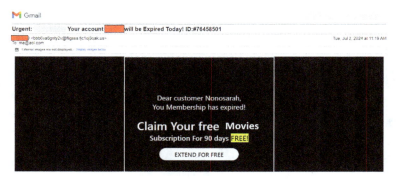

FIGURE 9.2 Email phishing example.

Table 9.2 describes the kinds of general categories of crime types that can be used to attack your computers and smart phones. Figure 9.3 is an image that describes this process.

TABLE 9.2 Cybercrime general categories

Crimes *against* computing devices	Crimes *using* computing devices
viruses	phishing emails
malware	spear phishing
ransomware	smishing
denial of service attacks (DOS)	cyberstalking
	identity theft
	Social engineering (this can also be accomplished without a computer via a telephone call or message or even through a letter)

FIGURE 9.3 What a data attack can look like.

Regular Data Backups

In today's world, almost every picture taken, and every communication made is done on a computer or cell phone. More than half the world's Internet users access the Internet from a smartphone. When computing devices fail either by accident or due to malicious activity, family pictures of deceased loved ones, business documents, schoolwork, and so on are all gone unless the data was backed up. The most important measure to take to insure one recovers from data disasters is adopting procedures for creating regular backups that were discussed in Chapter 8.

THE IMMEDIATE CYBER-RESPONSE

Table 9.3 is a checklist that includes FBI general guidelines for dealing with an attack on a computer system with a few additional suggestions. More information from the FBI can be found at *https://www.fbi.gov/investigate/cyber#What-You%20 Should%20Know* and *https://www.fbi.gov/how-we-can-help-you/scams-and-safety/ common-scams-and-crimes/ransomware*

Ransomware Attacks

This book has repeated stressed to keeping operating systems, software (including sure antivirus and antimalware) and applications current and up to date, and data backup procedures, and not clicking on links or making questionable downloads. All these steps are also FBI recommendations for preventing ransomware attacks along with creating a contingency plan in case of an attack. The FBI position does not support paying ransom. They note:

> Paying a ransom doesn't guarantee you or your organization will get any data back. It also encourages perpetrators to target more victims and offers an incentive for others to get involved in this type of illegal activity. If you are a victim of ransomware contact your local FBI field office to request assistance, or submit a tip online. File a report with the FBI's Internet Crime Complaint Center (IC3). (Federal Bureau of Investigation, n.d.) Figure 9.4 is an example of a message a computer might display during a ransomware attack.

```
> WHAT HAPPEND?

Important files on your network have been ENCRYPTED and now have the extension .DHBGDIGHII.
To recover your files, you need to follow the instructions below.

> SENSITIVE DATA

Sensitive data from your network has been DOWNLOADED.
If you DON'T WANT to your sensitive data PUBLISHED on our leak blog, you must act quickly.

LEAK BLOG: noescapemsqxvird                                    ad.onion

Data includes:
- Personal data of employees, resume, DL, SSN.
- Complete network map, including credentials for local and remote services.
- Private financial information including: customer data, accounts, budgets, annual reports, bank statements.
- Production documentation, including: datagrams, diagrams, drawings.
- And much more...

Sample DOWNLOADED FILES are available in your user panel.

> CAUTION

DO NOT MODIFY ENCRYPTED FILES BY YOURSELF.
DO NOT USE THIRD PARTY SOFTWARE TO RESTORE YOUR DATA.
YOU MAY DAMAGE YOUR FILES, THIS WILL RESULT IN PERMANENT DATA LOSS.

> WHAT SHOULD I DO NEXT?

You need to contact us:
1. Download and install TOR browser: https://www.torproject.org/
2. Go to your user panel:
bwjbbpbcihg                              taid.onion/9a85ac1f-b323-       -a142d3cd887e

If you have difficulties with authorization in the client panel, you can use the contact form in the "LEAKS BLOG" to
contact us
```

FIGURE 9.4 Example ransomware note on a computer.

In Table 9.3 we have provided a checklist of considerations if you become a victim of a ransomware attack. Review this before an attack so you can have an idea of the kinds of things you need to accomplish of you ever do become a ransomware victim.

TABLE 9.3 Cyberattack Response Checklist

Action	Date	Notes
Isolate all potentially infected computers. This means removing all the possibly infected devices from the network. This will prevent any further exposure to the network. Physically discount the network cable from the computer or turn off Wi-Fi on the device.		
Power off any other devices.		
Immediately secure backup data or systems by taking them offline.		
Change online account passwords and network passwords.		
Review logs. Computers and networks servers have logs of the computer's and users' actions. Reviewing these logs can provide information about the extent of the attack. IT support assistance may be needed to find and interpret these logs		
Get help from local IT support as needed.		
Warn family, friends, and associates about the possible attack.		
Contact kaw enforcement (Chapter 6, see Table 6.9)		
Contact the ISP, social media, or Web site involved.		
Close affected accounts		

RESPONDING TO CYBER HARASSMENT

Don't engage: Don't react to the harasser, don't respond or reply to messages or posts, simply do not acknowledge the person's existence. Online harassers generally only want a reaction from the user. Getting none most likely will stop their activity.

Block: Take the proper measures to prevent this person from contacting the user on the service. Most social media services have some way to block contact.

Report them: Notify the Web service they contacted the user on, and if needed, contact law enforcement.

Checking for spyware: This is a little trickier, but make sure antivirus software is up to date. If the user still thinks there is an issue with their phone or computer (the stalker has hacked the user's device), stop using it, change accounts, and get a new phone or computer. If things get worse, consider consulting with an expert on digital hacking. Beware some stalkers may leave a tracking device in their victim's vehicle or person. Seek law enforcement assistance if this is suspected.

What to do if they show up in real life: Call 911 if it's an emergency. If the user can't escape the location, go somewhere safe, then call 911.

CONTACTING LAW ENFORCEMENT

If the police don't know the crime occurred, there is nothing they can do to assist the user. The case may seem minor, but reporting it lets the authorities know a criminal is at work. The user's report, even if it's minor, may provide necessary information to further law enforcement investigations. Other things to consider include:

1. Always contact law enforcement if someone is in immediate danger.

2. Reporting the loss to your insurance company often requires a police report number.

3. Contact the companies and banks where the fraud occurred.

4. Place fraud alerts through all the credit reporting agencies and ask for credit reports.

REPORTING A CYBERCRIME

Chapter 6 (this volume; Tables 6.9 and 6.10) provides law enforcement contacts for reporting cybercrimes. Law enforcement will require a variety of information that points to the activities who, what, where, when, and why. The following is the information that may be required to make a report.

Documentation

Documentation is evidence law enforcement can use to commence an investigation and a picture is worth 1,000 words. It is suggested to take screen shots of the incident with one important exception. If the report is about a site or person that is accused of human trafficking or specifically shows appalling images of children in a sexual context, do not *copy them, screenshot them,* or *save them to a computer* or *other media.* Doing so may be violating the same law that is being reported. Take notes that identify the site location and/or who posted. For instructions on taking screen shots see Windows, Mac, Smartphone, or do a Google search for *the user's specific device + screenshot.* Figure 9.5 uses the Facebook Group, *The Cyber Safety Guys,* to give the user the important focus areas. It will likely require taking several screenshots to make sure all information is captured. Be aware of where the screenshots are being saved, as they are going to be needed later. If the user can't take screenshots, consider printing the material out. The user also might take digital pictures of the material.

Sometimes additional steps are required. For instance, an embedded URL in a link in a phishing email will not show up in a screenshot or printout. Capturing this link without clicking on it may be difficult. The simplest is to hover the user's mouse cursor over the suspect link, and it will open a small screen showing the link. The user can then take a screenshot of the link or write it down.

Who: Collection efforts should include the author or source of the information. This may require the user to look at the user profile and capture it alongside a troubling post. Emails will have to be expanded to show header info. Revealing the header information is different for each email client. If the user wants more information on finding the header information in their email, they can go to MX Toolbox's Web site at *https://mxtoolbox.com/Public/Content/EmailHeaders/.* They have a detailed list of email clients and how to access the headers.

Email headers contain tracking information for an individual email which is useful for law enforcement. They detail the route a message took across the Internet as it was passed through the various mail servers (called mail transfer agents) from the sender to the receiver. This can be one or two mail servers, or several more depending on the route taken and the email services used (Gmail to Gmail accounts never leave Google's servers). These email headers, in addition to the server's information, also contain time stamps (when the server passed on the email), IP addresses (of that server), sender/recipient information, and other potentially useful information for investigators. This information helps assist law enforcement to find and locate the person who sent the email.

Why/What: Posts might be text, a picture, and/or video. Be prepared to describe why the user believes it warrants action beyond just providing the screenshots. Law enforcement may not have time to review the video or images without some specifics of why the user believes it is suspicious or illegal. For instance, the video provided reflects a person discussing threatening to harm or kill someone.

Where: Sometimes, a post will include information that reflects where the author is located or maybe who their intended target is. If the user can ascertain that from the post, document it. When in cyberspace, it is important to provide an *address* of where the post was seen. In Figure 9.5, it is clear from the screenshot that it was viewed on Facebook, particularly as it includes the URL. One needs to get the entire address, not just the domain name. Sometimes, it is not clear from the screenshot. Maybe the post occurred in a chatroom or instant message. The user might have to write it down if they can't get the location documented in the screenshot. Again, be complete in documentation.

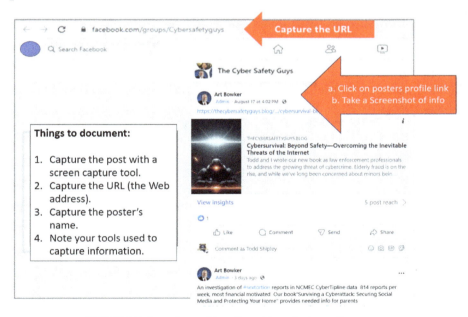

FIGURE 9.5 Capturing usable online evidence for law enforcement.

When: The user has taken screenshots, printed them out, or taken digital pictures. Maybe it includes the date and time, but maybe not. The user needs to document when they saw it, that is, the date, time, and their time zone. Go *old school* and write it down. For instance, the post was seen at the date/time/time zone at this cyberlocation (specific complete URL, specific chat, specific instant message, etc.)

Reporting the Crime

Documentation, including screenshots, has been made. Now, it is time to report. *Clearly, if this is in the user's area and is an emergency, call 9–1–1.* Explain what you saw and saved and why the user thinks it warrants attention. Be prepared to provide copies of screen shots, printouts, pictures, and documentation to law enforcement electronically via email or a storage device. Find the appropriate law enforcement contact listed Chapter 6 of this book and report the crime.

CREDIT MONITORING VERSUS FREEZING

Credit Monitoring

Credit monitoring is a service that tracks changes in an individual's borrowing behavior. It intended to notify the user of potential fraud using their name and credit and any changes to their creditworthiness that could be caused by fraud. Monitoring does not prevent fraud, but it can alert the user that it is possibly occurring.

A user can begin monitoring their own credit by requesting a free copy of their credit report (*https://www.annualcreditreport.com/*). In the United States, the three credit bureaus are required by law to provide an individual a copy if requested. Contact the user's bank and credit card companies and set up notifications to alert on transactions that might indicate fraud on the user's account. This could be withdrawals, or purchases that exceed a specified amount, or other activity not normal for the user's account and history.

If the user does not reside in the United States, they will have to do a little research on the Internet to determine the exact resources and companies available for this service. Credit bureaus operating outside the United States offer similar services. This *Business Insider* link can give users a start *https://www.businessinsider. com/credit-score-around-the-world-2018-8#2-united-kingdom-2*.

Credit Freeze

A credit freeze is a method used to protect consumers from identity theft. It is a request to one or more of the credit bureaus to *not* share the user's credit information with any third parties. In other words, if someone tries to get access to the user's information for the purpose of obtaining credit from a business, access will be denied. Table 9.4 provides the reader with an outline of the Credit Freeze concept.

TABLE 9.4 Credit Freezes

Who can place one:	Anyone can freeze their credit report, even if their identity has not been stolen.
What it does:	A credit freeze restricts access to the user's credit report, which means the user—or others—won't be able to open a new credit account while the freeze is in place. A user can temporarily lift the credit freeze if they need to apply for new credit. When the freeze is in place, the user will still be able to do things like apply for a job, rent an apartment, or buy insurance without lifting or removing it.
Duration:	A credit freeze lasts until the user remove it.
Cost:	Free
How to place:	In the United States, contact any of the three credit bureaus—Equifax, Experian, and TransUnion.

Fraud Alerts

A fraud alert is a security alert placed on an account. It usually references a credit card account or an account listing by a credit bureau. An alert is placed either by the customer, the credit card company, or the credit bureau when a possible fraudulent account activity is identified. Fraud alerts are available in different situations and have different benefits. Table 9.5 provides the reader with an outline of the Fraud Alert concept.

TABLE 9.5 Fraud Alerts

Who can place one:	Anyone who suspects fraud can place a fraud alert on their credit report.
What it does:	A fraud alert will make it harder for someone to open a new credit account in the user's name. A business must verify the user's identity before it issues new credit in their name. In the United States, when placing a fraud alert on a user's credit report, the user can get a free copy of their credit report from each of the three credit bureaus.
Duration:	A fraud alert lasts one year. After a year, the user can renew it.
Cost:	Free
How to place:	In the United States, contact any of the three credit bureaus—Equifax, Experian, and TransUnion. The user doesn't have to contact all three. The credit bureau contacted must tell the other two to place a fraud alert on the user's credit report.

Extended Fraud Alert

An extended fraud alert is a notification that appears on the user's credit reports for seven years. It asks lenders to verify the user's identity before processing credit or loan applications. The extended fraud alert was designed for identity theft victims to add a more extended period of protection on their credit history. The alert requires more information from the victim, and generally requires the submission of a law enforcement report to verify the status as an identity theft victim. Table 9.6 provides the reader with an outline of the Extended Fraud Alert concept.

TABLE 9.6 Extended Fraud Alerts

Who can place one:	An extended fraud alert is only available to people who have had their identity stolen and completed an FTC identity theft report at IdentityTheft.gov or have filed a police report.

Three Major Credit Bureaus Freeze Services

In the United States the credit bureaus work independently and require that each one is contacted to add alerts. Table 9.7 is a listing of the contact information the user can use to set up an alert. Table 9.8 is a listing of the contact information for credit bureaus outside of the United States.

TABLE 9.7 U.S. Credit Bureau Contact Information

Credit bureaus	Contact information
Experian	Online: Experian Freeze Center *https://www.experian.com/freeze/center.html* Phone: 1-888-397-3742 By mail, write to: Experian Security Freeze PO Box 9554 Allen, TX 75013
Equifax	Online: Equifax Credit Report Services *https://www.equifax.com/personal/credit-report-services/* Phone: 1-800-685-1111 By mail, write to: Equifax Information Services LLC PO Box 105788 Atlanta, GA 30348-5788
TransUnion	Online: TransUnion Credit Freezes *https://www.transunion.com/credit-freeze* Phone: 1-888-909-8872 By mail, write to: TransUnion LLC PO Box 2000 Chester, PA 19016

TABLE 9.8 Credit Bureaus Outside the United States

Credit bureaus	Contact information
GURU Inc. Global Links to Credit Reporting Agencies Credit	*https://www.creditguru.com/index.php/links-global-credit-agencies-collection-agencies*
European Credit Bureaus S&P Global, Moody's and Fitch, the so-called "Big Three" credit ratings agencies, are maintaining their dominance of Europe's credit score market.	*https://www.openriskmanual.org/wiki/European_Credit_Bureaus*

PERSONAL CYBER INSURANCE

A cyber insurance policy can provide reimbursement for the costs associated with the theft of digital information. Deciding if this kind of insurance is needed depends on what the user thinks the loss of their personal information can mean to them. A simple search on a favorite search engine can find the few companies offering this kind of insurance. These kinds of insurance can offer a homeowner the following coverages: personal, extortion, or fraud.

- *Personal protection coverage:* Protects against the financial costs of personal online attacks.

- *Cyber extortion:* Protects when online criminals threaten to expose personal data, photographs, or messages in return for a ransom of money or cryptocurrency.

- *Cyber financial loss:* Protects when a fraud of some kind occurs against the victim, such as fraudulent use of credit cards or identity theft.

- *Data breach:* Protects when personal data entrusted to the user is lost, stolen, or published, such as volunteer nonprofit data or small business credit card information from buyers, a thumb drive, or personal computing device is stolen.

CONCLUSION

This chapter covers a lot of information on what to do to survive a cyberattack. This is sometimes a complex and difficult task. With the things covered in this chapter and in other chapters of this book, the user should be able to limit the damage from the attack and work on recovery. Chapter 10 discusses what the future may hold.

REFERENCES

Federal Bureau of Investigation. n.d. "How to Respond and Report." Ransomware. FBI, n.d. *https://www.fbi.gov/scams-and-safety/common-scams-and-crimes/ransomware*

CHAPTER 10

FUTURE TRENDS

IN THIS CHAPTER

This chapter discusses future cyberconcerns and what can be done to prevent being a victim.

PREPARING FOR THE FUTURE

Proper preparation for surviving a cyberattack requires maintaining some awareness of future threats. This chapter focuses on two technologies, artificial intelligence (AI) and facial recognition, that the authors believe will increasingly be used to victimize the unprepared.

The Basics

Malware criminals constantly develop new viruses/worms and spyware to overcome a user's protection efforts. Chapters 2 and 3 covered the importance of keeping current on all updates to systems, applications, and antimalware software. These remain the basic steps in stopping a cyberattack against our systems in its tracks.

Keeping software and systems updated is just one aspect of being prepared. The user should also consider keeping up with news related to cyberevents. Both authors were victims of the 2015 United States Office of Personnel Management (O.P.M.) breach. The news alerted the authors of this breach weeks before O.P.M. officially notified us our data was included in the breach. For various reasons, some companies must be more ethical when providing client notifications. Trusted news sources can alert users ahead of the company notification. It can also be beneficial to regularly visit sites such as the Internet Crime Complaint Center (IC3) (*https://www.ic3.gov/Home/ConsumerAlertsChoice*), Krebs on Security (*https://krebsonsecurity.com*), and The Kim Komando Show (*https://www.komando.com/*) for cybercrime trends.

Artificial Intelligence (AI)

One of the most significant future cybercrime concerns is artificial intelligence (AI). A 2023 Presidential Executive Order on artificial intelligence provides the following definition:

> (b) The term "artificial intelligence" or "A.I." has the meaning outlined in 15 U.S.C. 9401(3): a machine-based system that can, for a given set of human-defined objectives, make predictions, recommendations, or decisions influencing real or virtual environments. Artificial intelligence systems use machine- and human-based inputs to perceive real and virtual environments; abstract such perceptions into models through analysis in an automated manner; and use model inference to formulate options for information or action. [Executive Order 2023, 15 USC 9401: Definitions [b]]

AI promises to solve all kinds of societal problems, including but not limited to disease cures and engineering problems. Current AI has limitations, but these limitations will likely be overcome with technological advances. The question is how quickly and whether humans control the advances or whether the AI controls its own advancement.

AI promises cybercriminals, either individuals or organizations, a powerful new tool to commit cyberattacks and make them more effective. AI can be adopted for cybercrime in several ways. As a direct tool, it can be used to find errors or exploits in software code. It can then be used to create viruses or worms that exploit those exploits.

It can also be used to find vulnerabilities in a company's cyberdefenses and overcome them. Cybercriminals can also use AI to pick the best targets for their attacks, be they companies to exploit or the most vulnerable and/or profitable targets for fraud schemes.

The law-abiding will use AI to make their software and defenses more secure. It then becomes an arms race of sorts with whose AI is better. The race's winners will be those with the resources to obtain the best AI. Companies will often be up against criminal organizations sponsored by their country's resources. The small business owner's odds could be better in this battle. The options they have are going to be those practices we mentioned in Chapters 8 and 9 for dealing with the aftermath. The private citizen likewise must be prepared to implement those practices mentioned in Chapter 9 for surviving an AI cyberincident of a victim entity that has their data.

AI also provides cybercrime criminals with a powerful social-engineering tool to overcome a victim's reluctance and gain their trust. It can be used to make phishing email/texting messages more believable. AI can generate images and videos that seem very real. They can fabricate pictures and videos of real individuals, including celebrities, to make their sales pitches more legitimate. They can convert images or videos of themselves, changing their age, race, and gender, and interact with their target in real time. It can be used to create fake voices, even in real time, for fraudulent phone schemes. These fake voices can even impersonate individuals the victim knows. It also allows one person to create multiple fake individuals to further sell their scheme. Not only does this make criminal social engineering more effective, it also further conceals their identity.

The protections noted in this book about never forwarding anyone's identifiers or banking information are the best defense. People should not invest in any scheme with someone they meet online, no matter how good it seems. They should make direct, independent contact with banks or other institutions before taking any action.

A Cybercriminal at Work

In the 2000s, a convicted bank robber and registered sex offender obtained a profile on the dating site Plenty of Fish. With this profile, he met an older female, gained her trust, and unlawfully obtained her credit card information. He used the credit card information to purchase a computer system illegally.

With the computer, he created a fictitious business. Using the knowledge he had gained while in prison, creating the warden's annual report, he created a fake company prospectus. Using the computer, he opened an Internet voice mail with different extensions. Anyone calling the number at the prompt would be presented with options for connecting with various departments, such as sales, engineering, and so on. He owned the company and was looking for investors.

Going back online and using his Plenty of Fish profile, he presented himself as a business owner with a PhD degree in engineering. He connected with a different older female who was married. He gained her trust and got her to cash out her 401(k) to invest in his fictitious company. The man was caught after the first victim reported his credit card fraud, and his scheme was detected through a review of his seized computer. He was sent back to prison.

His arrest and imprisonment were all done before AI. Imagine what this one criminal could have accomplished had he had access to AI to commit his fraudulent activity. AI will change the speed at which criminals can produce a fraudulent scheme. Law enforcement's challenge will be to keep up with those rapid advancements when criminals use AI.

Detecting AI in Use

There are programs to determine if AI was used, particularly for text. A simple Google search will reveal them. One suite of tools, Google Cloud's Vision AI (*https://cloud.google.com/vision*) can be used to analyze and detect AI-created material (text, images, and videos), but it is not free. There are other options for those who cannot invest in such programs. The Better Business Bureau (B.B.B.) has tips for detecting AI use in text, photos, and video (*https://www.bbb.org/all/spot-a-scam/how-to-identify-ai*)

AI is progressing, so errors and red flags in AI-generated content will likely be reduced. As technology evolves, tips for identifying problematic content will also change. Stay vigilant against fake videos and images by fact-checking before believing. Consider using SIFT, a four-step process for detecting manipulation [Caulfield 2019]. The SIFT steps are: *Stop, Investigate* the source, *Find* better coverage, and *Trace* claims, quotes, and media back to the original context.

Stop

In Stop, the user pauses and considers their knowledge of the Web site or information source, their reputation for being factual, and the claim being made. If the user does not have that knowledge, further research on the topic is suggested. Caulfield [2019] notes:

> Second, after you begin to use the other moves, it can be easy to go down a rabbit hole, going off on tangents only distantly related to your original task. If you feel yourself getting overwhelmed in your fact-checking efforts, STOP and take a second to remember your purpose. If you just want to repost, read an interesting story, or get a high-level explanation of a concept, it's probably good enough to find out whether the publication is reputable. If you are doing deep research of your own, you may want to chase down individual claims in a newspaper article and independently verify them. Please keep in mind that both sorts of investigations are equally useful. Quick and shallow investigations will form most of what we do on the Web. We get quicker with the simple stuff in part so we can spend more time on the stuff that matters to us. But in either case, stopping periodically and reevaluating our reaction or search strategy is key. (para. 7)

Investigate the Source

Who is presenting the information? Do they have an agenda or bias for presenting the information in a particular manner? Caulfield [2019] notes: "Taking sixty seconds to figure out where media is from before reading will help you decide if it is worth your time, and if it is, help you to understand its significance and trustworthiness better" (para. 11).

Find Better Coverage

Look for other sources of information beyond the initial reporting site. Focus on sites that are trusted for reporting and analysis. Develop a consensus from these other sources on whether the information initially presented is accurate.

Trace claims, quotes, and media back to the original context

Often, what is seen online has been reposted or forwarded from another site. Go back to where the original post was made. Tracing a claim, quote, etc., back to the original source can provide a sense of whether the version initially seen by the user was accurately presented.

FACIAL RECOGNITION

Facial recognition technology has evolved rapidly in recent years, enabling the identification and verification of individuals based on their facial features. This technology uses biometric data to identify individuals by analyzing their facial features and comparing them to a database of known faces. Its effectiveness has also been enhanced with AI. While it has many potential benefits, such as enhanced security and improved efficiency in law enforcement, it also has the potential to be misused by criminals. One of the most concerning ways facial recognition can be exploited is by stalkers and/or rapists, who could use the technology to identify, track, and target potential victims.

A Stalker's Dream

In the world today, social media and online platforms provide a treasure trove for criminals to obtain facial images of possible targets or identities to use in their crimes. The technology allows an attacker to take a picture of a potential victim in a public place and upload that picture to facial recognition sites. Upon doing so, the site may connect the photo to the victim's social media accounts, which can lead to the person's real name, address, and so on. This could lead to real-life stalking and potential harm to the victim.

Facial recognition software can also help collect photos of an actual individual. The collection is then used to support a fake profile, which is used to target others for fraud or worse. In this manner, photos of real individuals (often adult entertainment stars) are collected in various settings and used to create bogus profiles on dating sites.

CONCLUSION

The future of crime is bound to change drastically with continuous technological advancements. With the widespread use of AI, big data, and IoT, criminals will have access to more sophisticated tools to carry out their illegal activities. In addition, the rise of cryptocurrencies and other digital forms of money will make it easier for criminals to launder money and hide their tracks. There will continue to be increases in cybercrime as criminals become more adept at exploiting vulnerabilities in technology and targeting unsuspecting victims.

By leveraging predictive analytics and machine learning, law enforcement agencies can be able to identify crime patterns and predict potential criminal behavior. Real-time surveillance and facial recognition software will also aid in tracking suspects and solving crimes. This is happening in Europe and China. Smart cities could also play a role in reducing crime. Integrating technology in urban areas will allow for the advancement of security measures, including automated facial recognition and biometric identification systems. This could potentially deter criminals and make identifying and tracking them easier. Even such things as the use of blockchain technology could create a tamper-proof system for storing evidence and ensuring the integrity of data in legal proceedings. All of these technological changes must be balanced, particularly in the Western world, between individual privacy rights and the needs of the government to solve crimes. Technology isn't all bad. Methods and processes discussed in this book will prepare users to survive cyberthreats. It will be essential for society to stay vigilant and adapt to future changes to prevent and combat cybercriminal activities.

REFERENCES

Caulfield, M. (2019). "SIFT (The Four Moves)." Hapgood, June 19, 2019. *https://hapgood.us/2019/06/19/sift-the-four-moves/*

Executive Order No. 14110. "Safe, Secure, and Trustworthy Development and Use of Artificial Intelligence." Issued October 30, 2023.

https://www.whitehouse.gov/briefing-room/presidential-actions/2023/10/30/executive-order-on-the-safe-secure-and-trustworthy-development-and-use-of-artificial-intelligence/

INDEX

www.ingramcontent.com/pod-product-compliance
Lightning Source LLC
LaVergne TN
LVHW062318060326
832902LV00013B/2282